The Woman Who Took Back Her Streets

The Woman Who Took Back Her Streets

One Woman Fights The Drug Wars And Rebuilds Her Community

by

Rita Webb Smith
and
Tony Chapelle

NEW HORIZON PRESS
Far Hills, New Jersey

Library of Congress Catalog Card Number: 90-53581

Rita Webb Smith and Tony Chapelle
  The Woman Who Took Back Her Streets

ISBN: 0-88282-065-6
New Horizon Press

Dedication

This book is dedicated to the memory of my parents,
Alfrieda Dias Webb and David Webb,
to my aunt, Camily Richards,
and the reasons for it all, my children,
Judy, David, Mark, Gladys, Peter, Ayana and Abena.

Acknowledgments

We wish to thank our many friends and supporters, both past and present: Gertrude Russell, Marie Alvarenga, Ann Ashford, Frances Stitt, Florence Rice, Daisy Coleman, Emily White, Dora Little, Ruth Collins, John Coster, Dorothy Day, Norman Larche, Reverends Gatewood and MacMurray, Helen Baldwin, Ruth Tudos, Cyril Hunt and Ethel Gaynor.

The following organizations supplied support without which the fight could never have succeeded: Alpha Kappa Alpha Sorority, Zeta Phi Beta Sorority, Delta Sigma Theta, the American Muslim Mission, Nation of Islam, Mosque of Islamic Brotherhood, Utility Club, Central Harlem Democratic Club, New York Association of Black Psychologists, Citizens Action For a Safer Harlem, Howard University, Marymount University, Mother African Methodist Episcopal Zion Church, Mt. Calvary Methodist Church, Congress of Racial Equality, Tappan School, Countee School, the 32nd Precinct Council, Harlem Fight Back, Catholic Worker, Office of the Borough President, National Association of University Women, Phase Piggy Back, Inc., Harlem School of the Arts, National Association of Negro Business and Professional Business Women, American Red Cross (Harlem Branch), St. Thomas Liberal Catholic Church, Association of Black Social Workers, We Care New York Urban Coalition, Metropolitan Applied Research Center, Fordham University, Municipal Art Society, St. Charles Borromeo Church and School, Committee For Community Excellence, Concerned Citizens, Wonder Woman Foundation, Northside Center for Child Development, Emanuel Pieterson Historical Society, Office of the Mayor, Housing Preservation and Development, Office of the City Council and The People of Harlem.

Our Friends in the media: Earl Caldwell, Dick Ryan, Sidney Fields, Fred Noriega, Carol Martin, Poncietta Pierce,

Childrens' Express, Nice People, This Is Your Life, A Better Way, The People and Cedric McClester.

The New City Police Department 32nd Precinct: Inspector Joseph Vincent, Inspector Louis Anemone, Lieutenant Peter N. Pranzo, the Street Conditions Unit consisting of Gene Mullahy, Nicholas Marrazo, Walter Breslin, John Bailey, Harold Davis, James Davis, Frank Leissler, Joe Croon, Robert Smith, Louis LeBlanc, Edward Haas and Steven Rubino, the Special Narcotics Enforcement group of Norman Finkelstein, Thomas Drogan, Michael Libretto, Robert Dimarco, Michael Avellone, Louis D'Erocole, Craig Moruzzi, Larry Mikoleski, Frank Bifulco, Robert Kryger, Louis Manetta and Robert Sobociensk.

And our good friends in Community Relations, Walter Williams, Onnie Grier, Alwin Mayers, Marvin Blue and Ella Owens.

And a special thanks to Richard Curtis, our agent, who believed and persevered.

Contents

Introduction: America's Most Populous Block
Prologue: A Brother Intervenes

Introduction: America's Most Populous Block

143rd Street and Harlem for that matter didn't always have a war zone atmosphere. In the twenties when Duke Ellington arrived to play jazz at the Cotton Club, he was thrilled by the sight of a Harlem Street he said looked "just like the Arabian Nights." An astounded Cab Calloway, a few years later, said he "had never seen a street as glamorous as Seventh Avenue", the same street which became the drug battle ground of America.

Black people had been living in Manhattan since 1626 when eleven Africans were brought in servitude to the Dutch settlement of New Amsterdam (which became New

York). During the years that followed a majority of black people living in Manhattan inhabited the west side. By 1900 crowded housing, pressure by incoming white groups and finally the race riot of 1905 in the San Juan Hill district caused many black families to pack up their belongings in horse drawn vans and wagons and migrate uptown to Harlem.

At this time Harlem, *Haarlem* in Dutch, was inhabited mostly by whites of European heritage. Well appointed brownstones, deluxe apartments and row houses such as the exclusive enclave designed by renowned architect Sanford White Strivers Row, where beige terra cotta facades were said to be reminiscent of the Florentine Renaissance, were interspersed with an occasional mansion complete with stables and manicured lawns. In the row houses lived architect Vertner Tandy who designed St. Phillips Episcopal Chapel. Charles Roberts, Wiley Wilson, and other professional people such as businessmen and state politicians lived in this affluent setting. The school their children attended, Grammar School 68, was nicknamed "the Silk Stocking School of the City."

Some of those "in the upper crust" lived in the Sugar Hill district, a neighborhood where those like NAACP's director Walter White and entertainers Bill "Bojangles" Robinson, Duke Ellington and Cab Calloway had homes. The majestic Italian stoneworks carved into the shapes of lions heads decorating these buildings on Sugar Hill's Edgecombe Avenue were comparable to those on the more famous Riverside Drive, Fifth Avenue or Park Avenue. Splendid, high ceiling residences such as the Florence Mills Apartments overlooked a steep bluff that afforded breathtaking views of the city. Block after block of luxurious four story homes with tall bay windows graced Sugar Hill. On Convent Avenue was the Hamilton House where Alexander Hamilton had once lived.

On Seventh Avenue and 150th Street, you would have entered the exotically gardened and stone benched court-yard of the Paul Laurence Dunbar Apartments. John D. Rockefeller, Jr. had helped finance this five hundred and eleven apartment complex where notables such as actor Paul Robeson, civil rights activist W. E. B. DuBoise and labor leader A. Phillips Randolph once resided. In 1979, the Dunbar Apartments were added to the National Register of Historic Places.

Rockefeller had great interest in helping black Harlemites, but he also had a paternal streak. When promi-nent black minister Adam Clayton Powell, Sr. decided to move his midtown congregation to Harlem, Rockefeller of-fered to help finance construction of an ambitious new tem-ple. Powell may have accepted the oil millionaire's benevo-lence save for the condition set by Rockefeller that he be seated on the church's board of trustees where he would have a say in the financial decisions of the church. Powell scoffed. He subsequently built the Abyssinian Baptist Church entirely from parishioner support. Not long after-ward, Abyssinian became the world's largest, and one of the best known Protestant congregations. Powell's son, Adam, Jr., used this base to become the second black congressman since Reconstruction.

Theaters and showplaces already lined Seventh Avenue and on West 125th Street the Harlem Opera House, Hurtig and Seamons Music Hall, the New Orpheum Theater and several movie theaters were soon located. In addition, plush department stores, jewelry boutiques, banks and restaurants abounded, along with gambling dens, saloons, poolrooms and dance halls and, of course, numerous churches.

Within a few years, white families, some for profit, others impelled by prejudice, began to abandon the area and when St. Phillips Protestant Episcopal Church moved into a new building on West 133rd Street and bought an entire row of apartment houses, this act heralded the future all black makeup of the community.

Seventh Avenue was the most intoxicating of Harlem's boulevards. During prohibition, behind fashionable facades, "The Great Black Way" swayed with the sounds of Duke Ellington, Fats Waller, Fletcher Henderson and Coleman Hawkins.

The Bamboo Inn on Seventh Avenue was the place to see bejeweled and bedecked Harlemites "high Harlem" as one writer said. The block between Lenox and Seventh Avenues became known as Jungle Alley because of its array of clubs such as The Clam House, Tillie's Chicken Shack, Pods, Jerry's and Mexico's. It was in one of these clubs, Monelte Moore's, that Billie Holiday, the famed blues singer, was discovered.

One of Harlem's four top nightclubs, Small's Paradise, was reputed to have the hottest show in town. Big band jams, exciting floor shows and waiters who danced the Charleston as they served tables sparked the excitement. Nearby Barron Witkins where Duke Ellington played, catered, according to him "to big spenders, gambling sportsmen and women, all at the peak of their professions." Two blocks down Connie's Inn, said comedian Jimmy Durante, was the swankiest of Harlem's night spots.

During these same years a quieter but more far reaching political drive had begun in Harlem. The Universal Negro Improvement Association led by Marcus Garvey, a leading spokesman for black pride, separatism, and a return to Africa; as well as socialists such as A. Randolph Chandler Owens and others strove for economic reform. When these movements faded, an artistic resurgence, composed chiefly of poets, novelists and essayists such as Claude McKay, Countee Cullen, Langston Hughes, and James Weldon Johnson moved the social reform forward.

Meanwhile, the strength of Harlem's vast church network grew. James Weldon Johnson wrote "There are something like one hundred and sixty colored churches in Harlem." Indeed, major churches like the Abyssinian Baptist and St. Phillips Protestant Episcopal drew the well-off, but it was the storefront churches which drew the poor and uneducated, many of whom bore the worst economical hardships facing the country as well as the bitter intensity of social problems besetting the black race.

Though Harlem was called the Amusement Center of the world by *Variety*, by 1930 the effects of America's depression had hit Harlem hard. The theaters, ball rooms and night clubs were still throbbing to intoxicating beats as the rich tried to forget Wall Street's crash. "But there was five times as much unemployment in Harlem", according to *The New York Times*, "as in other parts of the city."

And nowhere was the depression more deeply felt than on America's most peopled block, West 143rd Street. The United States Census Bureau reported that this particular block was home to three thousand families, the largest number on any city block in America. New York City health officials, unfortunately, also referred to the street as "the lung block" during the 1930's because residents there died from pulmonary tuberculosis at twice the rate of white Manhattanites.

Although it was only one block off Seventh Avenue, 143rd Street was on the wrong side of that local economic dividing line in what was known as the Valley. Here, ubiquitous tenement houses were crowded so close that the street appeared to be one long wall of apartment exteriors. Rickety fire escapes zig-zagged down the red brick faces of these buildings which were usually five to seven stories tall. At the edge of the sidewalk there were always waist-high heaps of trash waiting for the city garbage trucks.

Inside these buildings lived Harlem's sober, hardworking core, most of whom never saw the flashy nightlife indulged in by the small percentage of high livers. After the depression the median income of a Harlem family fell to $1019.00. Yet more and more black Americans migrated to Harlem. 143rd Street bulged, overflowing with the new migrants. As the depression continued and America's average income fell, those who had been Harlem's poor; teachers, social workers, pullmen, porters and red caps—those who had fixed but modest incomes were termed "the rising proletariat."

It was on this block and into this post-depression social and economic climate that Rita Webb Smith was born. In childhood Harlem seemed to her encircled by world-renowned playspots. Her own block was sandwiched between Yankee Stadium, staring down at her from the Bronx, and the swinging Savoy Ballroom where her parents shook their hips on more than a few nights.

Though tenement housing was crowded, life on the block was exciting, especially for children. An army of friends were forever jumping double-dutch, playing poxie, a game which everywhere else is called hopscotch, hiding and seeking or berating each other in a game called dumb school. Kids climbed the fence to the park across the street after it closed at five o'clock. The same man who managed the park, Ollie Edinborough, a man who knew that kids need company, is still a resident of the neighborhood. For Rita Webb Smith those were delightful times.

During Harlem's glory period, Cab Calloway had also frequented the block, although he didn't live there. Good-looking and well-dressed, Cab used to stride through the neighborhood on his way to the Cotton Club at Lenox Avenue and 142nd Street where he made his mark on American entertainment with his gymnastic bandleading and his trademark phrase, "Hi De Ho."

Althea Gibson, the international tennis champion, grew up on this same block. Althea was the first black person to ever win at Wimbledon or to capture the United States Open championship. When she was named Woman Athlete of the Year in 1958, her picture was on the cover of *Time* Magazine. Althea was tall and competitive. As a child she played tennis on "summer street", a street closed off to car traffic by the Police Athletic League to let children frolic all day long.

Because of Althea, her father became somewhat of a celebrity in the neighborhood. One day he announced to his friends that his famous daughter was relocating the family from 135 West 143rd Street to a ten room house on Long Island. Those like Rita were sad and even a little envious that the family was leaving the neighborhood. She imagined them moving into a beautiful country home with trees and flowers and uncrowded sidewalks where they were sure to find peace and tranquility.

Besides Althea, there were more celebrity residents. Other notables from the block included rhythm and blues band, the Isley Brothers, and Isabel Sanford, later the TV wife of George Jefferson in the situation comedy series, "the Jeffersons." Isabel lived across the street at 106 West 143rd.

Then there was actor Charlie McGregor, who lived in building number 135, the same apartment house where Althea once resided. In 1972, Charlie played the role of Freddie the Junkie in the controversial movie "Super Fly." In the movie, which some black critics accused of glorifying a fictitious Harlem cocaine dealer, Charlie's drug addicted character came to a bitter end. It was a role that Charlie could well identify with: he had once been an addict himself, a fact he later wrote about in his autobiography, *Up From The Walking Dead* a book about his season of addiction.

Aside from this roster of stars however, the block was home to just common folk. To those who lived there during these years, the block offered a sense of security and a kind of extended family. Parents took responsibility for everyone's children.

Neighbors observing Rita as a small child would ask: "Does your mother know you're out here?" That was the kind of security the block afforded, the kind that covered Rita with warmth, like going to a friend's house to sneak a dinner when Rita's Momma, only hours before, had cautioned in her broken English, "Now Rita, don't eat at nobody's house. You make sure you wait 'til you come home."

Still parental guidemarks were strong within the community. Adults demanded that children behave, but grown-ups had a live-and-let-live attitude toward other adults and their interests. There was the local after-hours spot where you could get whiskey or wine at any time of the night. There was also a well-known businesswoman who ran a house of ill repute where all kinds of wild parties took place. Yet since these were camouflaged so that church-going folks on the block weren't blatantly offended, they were allowed to coexist with everyday community life.

On the one hand, you had people who religiously went to church every Sunday wearing white, but on the other hand, were rumored to have alcoholic problems midweek. Those people who had problems got support from the neighborhood in small ways, like maybe having someone look out for their children, or bring them food baskets.

During these days everyone knew the local numbers runners like Willie Roach, Teets and Joe Buford. Sometimes they would give "scholarships" to kids who were going to college. Besides the basic gift of money, the numbers men gave parents, especially single mothers, graduation dresses, shoes or other clothing for their children and when necessary, even trainfares to the destinations of their choices. In the Jet Age, they advanced to giving airfare. Ironically, despite earning illegitimate livelihoods, the numbers guys, unlike the later drug dealers, lived and worked on the block. Aside from their questionable business activities, they took a strong interest in the neighborhoods and their neighbors' well being.

Some of the neighbors came from the South, others from Africa and, just as Rita's parents, many people on the street had come from the Caribbean Islands. In fact, Rita learned to speak a French dialect from one of the children from Martinique, an island that had been a French possession. The dialect was not grammatically correct French, but a version similar to America's Black English.

That was 143rd Street, America's most populous block during Rita Webb Smith's childhood. The most colorful nostalgia of it she still fondly remembers. The violent reality of it she lived every day.

.

Prologue: A Brother Intervenes

*I*t was four o'clock, Friday, a steamy August afternoon. David felt mildly prosperous after putting in a day's work at the electrician's job, and he felt energized after jogging the Harlem streets from 143rd down to Central Park and back. He was on familiar turf now, right around the corner from his own apartment building.

Slowing down, he waved to four or five of his Muslim friends, his brothers as he called them, gathered outside the health food store a Muslim named Daoud owned at 665 Lenox Avenue. Daoud, which means David in Arabic, also owned the fish and chips store next door. He stood talking intently to the young men. Because the kids made him feel like one of them, Daoud didn't chase them away as the other store owners did.

Stopping to catch his breath, David saw his brother Peter among the group. "Hey man," he called out walking over and thumping his brother's back.

Peter shushed him. Daoud and David's friends had just joined in the daily "parliament," which is what they called waxing philosophical about Islam, Allah, their theory of creation, or just about being black in America. Rapping intently on the sidewalk in the sizzling hot of summer, they were suddenly interrupted by the commotion caused by a boy and a woman about thirty yards away, screaming obscenities and wrestling with each other.

At first David paid little attention. After all, this was Harlem 1979. Dozens of pushers operated a drug market on 143rd Street. Scramblers drummed up business. Some waited for customers on the corner, others loitered along the street or crouched on this stoop or in that doorway. They blatantly stood on the sidewalks and openly approached passersby whispering sales pitches like, "Make it on Black Sunday," a street code for heroin, or "Try sess," a shorthand for sensamilla, an exotic strain of marijuana.

The street pushing done on 143rd Street in 1979 was the same kind that eventually took over many American cities. The drug dealers in this neighborhood had been getting away with openly peddling dope and had been getting bolder at doing so for about a year. Easy money flowed, but so did blood. Many days someone was shot for selling dope on someone else's turf or because they had gone too long without paying for drugs bought on credit. In order to survive, one kept his distance.

As the boy and woman got closer, David recognized the boy's voice. Whirling around, David saw his younger brother Mark pushing a tall, unkempt woman towards them. The woman was trying to get loose, but Mark forced her up against a parked truck with one hand and shook a hammer in her face shouting, "My mama's told you, now I'm telling you, don't be hustling drugs in front of my house. Take your stuff and get outta here, ya understand?" Mark's other hand was fastened on her grimy collar while he craned his own neck to holler right in her face.

The woman, Cleo, was one they'd seen before. She was a touter, someone who stands on the street and directs heroin customers to drug dealers hawking in doorways and vacant lots. Dealers and their lookout people usually paid the touters with more of their white powder.

Cleo was more than a nuisance. She was a heroin addict and a promiscuous lesbian with designs on young girls. Up close she had teeth like Bugs Bunny, a dirty, uncared-for Afro and a caramel colored, acned complexion. Even though she stood slightly hunched over, she was very tall, maybe six feet, a height many a fashion model would envy. Cleo could have been able to mold herself a statuesque body had she ever been imbued with poise and self-worth. As it was, she was a user who wore the jeans and jackets common to the working class man.

As she and Mark struggled, David watched tensely while Sonny, part of the street's dope trade, slid off the white Cadillac on which he'd been perched and strode menacingly toward them. Sonny, his real name was Fred Figures, was a burly, bushy Afro-haired bodyguard who was supposed to insure that dealers and touters like Cleo weren't robbed. Up close Sonny's half-closed eyelids and trembling lips betrayed his identity as just another heroin addict.

All the guys in the parliament ran toward the fight, but David got there first. He stepped back and forth in front of Sonny, blocking him. "Mind your own business, man," David ordered.

The hood tried to push past, but David held him back. They tussled, grappling each other's shoulders like linemen playing football. When Sonny shoved a little too hard, David reacted to the threat. He gripped the bodyguard with his left hand, cocked back his right fist, and slammed a stiff jab into Sonny's face. It was a bull's eye; his fist met with all jaw.

Sonny stumbled backwards, pain quickened instincts born of years on mean streets. His mind registered the odds against him; he was outnumbered by his opponent's friends, and possibly outclassed by his opponent's physical power.

In the same adrenaline-charged thought, he obviously concluded that his reputation on the street could be irreparably undermined should word get around he had been successfully challenged. Pragmatism, bravado, fear, all boiled within him. Sonny reached into his black cotton golf jacket and snatched out a .38 caliber pistol. "Motherfucker, I'm going to kill you."

The sight of the gun startled David. He hadn't seen, nor bargained for, an equalizer. But, as Sonny pulled out the gun, David's mind quickly registered its caliber, its make and, most importantly, the damage it was capable of wreaking. The weapon, a Colt, had once been steel blue in color, but had faded to dirty gray. Although it was at least twenty years old, at this range even an old pistol could kill.

David was street wise. He had seen guns before. At age thirteen, he surreptitiously bought his first "piece" from a hard-up addict. He stared intently at Sonny and at the weapon in Sonny's hand. And, in that slow-motion second, the one which sometimes catalyzes life-threatening situations, David quickly decided that Sonny didn't know how to use his weapon. Any gunman worth his price, even one paid to protect drug pushers, pulls out a pistol and, without a second thought, cocks the hammer back with the side of his thumb so it doesn't slip. But Sonny imitated the histrionics of an old James Cagney gangster, lazily brandishing the .38 on its side, his palm facing the sky.

However, five feet was too far a chasm for David to lunge across to disarm Sonny. David hesitated. He turned and barely shifted his weight to run when he felt a sharp pain in the chin. He was already hit before he heard the shot.

David bolted for cover across the street where a half dozen people gathered around an outdoor table selling fruit. A prominent dope dealer named Gramps Tiler owned the fruit stand, and his mother and family sat out there. David figured his assailant wouldn't shoot in that direction. As inexperienced as Sonny was, he might hit Gramps Tiler's daughter or wife or mother. Then he'd have hell to pay.

Beyond the tables, David broke into a full run. He chanced a look over his shoulder. Sonny wasn't chasing him. Now David's only worry was what was up ahead. His chin felt numb, like he'd been punched. No burning or stinging. No taste. Nothing. David mumbled, "It's like I don't have a chin, like my whole lower jaw is gone."

From where he was running in the street, next to parked cars and moving vehicles, he could look downtown and see the one place he would be safe and where he could get medical attention. In the distance loomed the Empire State Building and the north end of the Manhattan skyline. But all David focused on among Lenox Avenue's converging lines of tenement apartments was an edifice six blocks away. Harlem Hospital.

At 142nd and Lenox he slowed down long enough to frantically hail a cab. Dark red blood splattered his chin, neck and hands. Blood ran down the front of his sweatshirt and stained his sweatpants. One of the omnipresent Harlem gypsy cabs sped closer and David jumped up and down trying to be seen. The cabbie saw the frightened young man bleeding like a wounded dog and obviously in trouble—just the kind of rider who endangers a cabbie and probably doesn't have sufficient fare. The cab never slowed down.

David figured no other driver would stop for him either. There was no sense in just standing there bleeding to death. He would have to make it to the hospital on foot.

WHO?
MISS RITA

1

Westerly Winds: Stories Told a Small Child

Darkness snuck into Harlem like a thief. Even before the streetlights went on, its furtive nightlife had begun. Strangers freely milled on the sidewalks waiting for either customers or a buy. Dealers hid in building hallways or watched from inside cars parked in dirt encrusted alleys or stashed in weed filled lots.

Although the young men and women congregated on door stoops flirting, touching, incessantly giggling, communicating those same secrets which have been eternally passed from one sexually budding generation to the next, most of the older people didn't venture out at

night except to visit Jerry's or one of the other nearby
bars. They were afraid to walk on streets where random
gunfire, senseless druggies and misdirected hits could
seek them out at any moment. Instead, they cowered
inside dimly lit apartments, peeking from behind thick
curtained windows.

Rita Webb Smith had always refused to be one of
these people. She lived her beliefs with bold strokes and
the pride she had been taught by her proud parents and
grandparents.

"*I* was born in Harlem Hospital.

"I could have been born in a million places other than
Harlem. But the warm, westerly winds that breathe over
the Atlantic Ocean nudged my ancestors across the Caribbean Sea urged by those fateful Gulf Stream breezes and
from there on to New York. The Atlantic, the Caribbean
Sea, and those fateful Gulf Stream winds played a role in
my family history, from the age of the great explorers right
on down to my parents' time. Some came bound in the
bellies of slave ships from Africa. Others booked passage
aboard merchant vessels from the Iberian peninsula. And,
ultimately, one of my parents arrived in New York by stowing away.

"My family is unusual in that, as African-Caribbeans
and then as African-Americans, we are still somewhat close
to the European side of our family. Black Americans are
obviously derived of African people. Some of us know a bit
about the Native American blood in our families. But few
African Americans have any knowledge about their ances-
tral tribes or homelands as their fourth or fifth generation
Anglo American, or German American counterparts proba-

bly have. Many of us also have some white forebears, although most have no idea who they were or where they came from.

"My family is a little different. While we, unfortunately, don't know any more about our African heritage than most blacks, we do know about our white relatives. We know, for instance, that they were not slaveholders. European slavemasters often had their way with young, helpless slave girls, and left progeny. But in my family, Europe and Africa mingled through old-fashioned mutual attraction.

"I was told about my African history as a little girl snuggled against my daddy on our big embroidered sofa. He told vivid stories of how he had traveled the world as a ship hand, and how our family before him had scratched out an existence from the Caribbean soil to survive. Slowly he was lighting a simmering sense of responsibility within me, that I couldn't be less than my best or else I'd be letting a lot of people down.

"What my mother recounted about my white family she told with a mixture of pain and pride. Since she didn't go into very much detail, it was her half-sister who filled in for me what is a rich family portrait. Aunt Camily, the one aunt I have who is still alive, lives in New York upon what I call "Slaves' Row," the street named Sylvan Terrace. It's a beautifully kept, cobblestone street of small, brick rowhouses in New York City's Washington Heights. Adjacent to the Jemel Mansion, Sylvan Terrace was once actually a street lined with slave quarters. Aunt Camily lives in one of those remodeled houses. Over the course of years, she and others in my family explained to me the history of my Caribbean-European family.

"My mother was born in 1896 on the Caribbean island

of St. Kitts, in a town called Basseterre. Half Portuguese and a mix between African and Indian, she was what people back then called a mulatto, and what some people today call a love child—and others label illegitimate. Her father's family originated in Portugal in the town of Santa de Serra.

"Four years before Columbus bumped into the Americas, Sea Captain Bartholomew Dias—who Grandfather said was our direct ancestor—became the toast of Europe after finding a long-sought ocean route around the southern tip of Africa. Dias christened that point of land Cabo Tormentoso, or stormy cape. A decade later another Portuguese sailor, Vasco da Gama, followed Dias' water trail and was the first European to sail his way to India. Da Gama's good fortune led him to rename Dias' discovery "The Cape of Good Hope," which is its name to this day.

"The Portuguese were avid explorers because of their vigorous mercantile economy. During the 1400s and 1500s, they scoured the world in search of gold and spices to trade. But after moving along the African coast for a number of years, the Portuguese began engaging in another, wildly lucrative form of merchandising, the slave trade. Portugal began the practice of bringing African slaves to Europe. It was the children of those Africans whom the Spanish first forced to work in the New World, in the Haitian mines.

"Victor Dias, my mother's father, was a merchant too. Sometime between 1893 and 1895, Victor and his three sisters left their family home and the familiar surroundings of Santa da Serra, and set sail for the West Indies, the Caribbean islands which the British, French, Danish, Spanish and Dutch colonized. With their superior weapons of war, the European armies first brutalized the indigenous Arawak and Ge-Pano-Carib, or Carib Indians, forcing them to submit to being robbed of their land. Then they tried to make slaves of the Indians, and when that didn't work, brought enslaved Africans to the islands. Finally, European settlers flocked there, thirsty for the profit they knew they could extract from the Caribbean's rich resources with the help of slave workers.

"Victor Dias and his sisters settled on the island of St. Kitts, a tiny, volcano-created point southeast of Puerto Rico in the Leeward or Eastern Caribbean Islands. The indigenous people once called the island Liamuiga. But when Christopher Columbus landed there (and on Nevis, the island just two miles away) on his second voyage to the Americas, he renamed it St. Christopher, after his patron saint. Great Britain settled St. Christopher, or St. Kitts as it was nicknamed, from 1623 to 1713, and then wrestled with France for ownership. By the time Victor Dias arrived, St. Kitts and Nevis were combined into a joint British colony.

"On St. Kitts, a twenty-three-mile long speck of mountains and shortgrass pastures, the enterprising Dias raised horses and acquired a sugar cane plantation. Victor also opened a rum shop or liquor store in the capital, coastal town of Basseterre, and a general store where my mother worked when she became old enough. Through his broad holdings, Victor Dias became wealthy. As a result, my mother was blessed with a very comfortable upbringing. Many years later, my mother introduced me to men who had come to New York, having once been stable boys for her father.

"According to Aunt Camily, early in his Caribbean prosperity Dias met a lovely island girl named Ann Fipps, my grandmother. Ann's was a racially mixed heritage, a

23

combination of African and Carib Indians. She was a beautiful woman whose long hair fell past brown shoulders. Meticulous in her appearance, she enjoyed dressing fashionably, complete with the elaborate lace hats and silk hoop dresses popular at the turn of the century. But she was also a fiery woman who stood up to anybody, my aunt said. She taught school.

"Men and women who emerge from different hemispheres may have unfamiliar customs, but passion is universal, and many European settlers became romantically involved with Caribbean women. In fact, St. Kittsians have a national holiday to honor one of their countrywomen who married a British admiral.

"For the women, there were pragmatic advantages. For instance, when they bore mulatto children as a result of these relationships, the white fathers often made sure that their offspring were not raised wanting, and sometimes even had them educated abroad.

"For a sojourning man who was discovering a whole new land, an entirely different culture, and a strange yet friendly new people, Ann Fipps must have been considered an exotic prize of a woman. Not only was she well educated, and not only did she match the European standards of beauty, this island woman had fire.

"Although Ann conceived Victor's child, after their initial blush of romance Victor made it clear to his dark lover that he wouldn't be marrying outside of his race and social class. They had a stormy relationship for a brief time after that. Then my grandmother's fierce pride dictated that, although she was pregnant, she end her affair with Victor.

"Ann soon gave birth to a baby girl, a child with the light green eyes and thin lips of her Iberian father and the straight nose and high cheekbones of her Carib-Afro mother. While nursing her infant for a week without coming outside, as was the custom for recently-delivered women, Ann fitfully waited in anticipation of a visit or word from her former lover. None came. She became infuriated by the scorn she perceived Dias was showing her. Even if he would not make them his family, the Portuguese gentleman farmer could at least send some gift to soften the hurt or money to help with expenses.

"Too, Ann probably feared she would not be able to remain a teacher and still care for a child. Nineteenth Century teachers were expected to be chaste, single, and examples of good character. When they married, or when their names buzzed too hotly on the gossip chains of small communities, they were usually dismissed. Instead of being free to fawn over her sweet-breathed infant, Ann Fipps was thus bedeviled with a heart full of cares.

"At the end of that fretful week, Ann bundled up their newborn baby and stormed out of her house. Finally she arrived at Victor Dias' general store and barged in. 'Victor was standing there at his big woodblock, chopping codfish for a customer,' my Aunt Camily said. 'He had his hand up, about to come down with the hatchet. And Ann quickly placed that week-old baby right there on the chopping block, right underneath where the blade was to fall. When he realized what was happening, Victor stopped short to keep from chopping the baby in two.

" 'This is your child,' Aunt Camily said Ann sobbed in her brusque English. 'Do with it what you will.' With tears streaming down her face, Ann Fipps turned on her heels and dashed out of the general store. Victor never saw her again.

"Made an instant caretaker, Victor had to find someone who could raise the child. Men almost never took on
the task of being sole parent to children in those days.
Victor turned to his sisters, Marie, Louisa and Jane, for
help. All had married mulatto men in St. Kitts. Jane had
married a minister named Rawlins. Together they agreed to
provide a caring family life for Victor's motherless daughter, my mother.

"With the help of a local nursing mother, the baby's
Aunt Jane reared the child and loved her with a passion.
Victor was apparently very affectionate toward her, too,
giving her lots of care, as well as his surname. She would be
known as Alfrieda Bonita Alethia Oyanto Dias.

"Despite her comfortable upbringing, Alfrieda did not
grow up in her father's household. So, my mother had very
ambivalent feelings toward her father, whom she loved and
resented at the same time.

"My grandfather Dias later married, not my grandmother, but a Portuguese woman. With his lawful wife, he
fathered two daughters, Louisa and Beryl Dias. They were
both raised there in Bassetere and played with my mother,
who grew up nearby almost as an oldest sister. But Aunt
Camily said my mother never liked them. When they grew
into women, my mother's half-sisters left St. Kitts. One
went to live in Brazil, the other to America. My grandfather
and his wife remained on the island. Later some other
members of the Dias family went to Georgetown, Trinidad,
and built a plant to make the formula for South American
angostura bitters. To this day, the Velasquez and Dias family are still running the business and distributing bitters all
over the world.

"When my mother reached marriageable age, my

grandfather wanted her to wed a man named Papo Gomes in St. Kitts. He had land and was a merchant. But Mama, like her mother, refused to marry a white man because she said she was black. She was a rebel in her way. Meanwhile, her mother Ann Fipps never married. She had three more children, my Aunt Camily, Blondina and Edwin. Like my grandfather, all of the men by whom Ann had children were white and a potpourri of European representation.

"Mother never knew her own mother very well. Ann died in her late twenties when she was riding in a wagon whose horse went over a cliff.

"My father's background was quite different from Momma's comfortable upbringing. He had a very difficult life, a life of deprivation and rejection. His father, George Webb, had been born a child of slaves on the island of Nevis sometime between 1845 and 1852. The slaveholder who once owned my family, James Webb, was the ancestor of the socialist Sidney James Webb who founded the London School of Economics and Political Science.

"My father, David Webb, used to sit me down some nights and weave, for my little girl's mind, stories that had been passed down to him about the African slaves. He explained the sufferings and the degradation of slave life. He spoke of the beatings. He explained how ashamed the women felt when they were hindered in passing on their language, culture and traditions to their children. For teaching their native languages to their children, the slaves would be beaten. I could always feel the pain when my father would tell me these stories.

"He told me how Christianity had been forced onto

slaves. 'I'm not a Christian, I'm a Muslin,' he kept repeating. My father spoke of how his father had been forced to accept Christianity, the slave masters and overseers making them pray each night under the threat of the whip. The prayer went like this: 'Mr. Mark, Mr. Luke, Mr. John, God bless the bed we lie upon.' Then with tears in his eyes, my father would explain that, 'the bed was made of hay.' Years later, my father told me that when I had heard his stories as a little girl, tears also came to my eyes.

"But Father's eyes would light up when he told the story about Emancipation Day in the islands. He said that when word got to the slaves that they'd been freed, they were overjoyed. They were so happy, he said, they broke out in songs. Apparently their pet name for the white man was 'Bakara,' which was an African term. So they sang, 'Emancipation bill done passed, and da' poor bakara has ta' eat nutgrass.'

"Although Britain decreed in 1833 that all slaves in its colonies would be set free, and most European states followed soon thereafter, the United States took much longer, until 1864, to emancipate its slaves. Part of the reason emancipation was accomplished much earlier in the British West Indies, for instance, was that the British House of Commons set aside the equivalent of $100 million to compensate slave owners. Without such financial incentive in America, southern slaveholders had to be put through a Civil War to give up slavery.

"When the British, the French, the Dutch and the Spanish had begun to colonize the Caribbean, they had never been able to force all of the fierce, indigenous peoples into slavery. Those who refused were of no value as chattel, and, since their presence represented a nuisance, the Carib and

Arawak peoples were poisoned. Their race almost died out, and the remnant was conquered. Just as in the United States, Europeans then imported Africans to the islands to farm the plantations and perform household tasks. Almost half of the two million African slaves brought to North America and the Caribbean colonies landed in the West Indies. In this region, which was much smaller than the United States, there were soon more blacks than any other nationality.   \

"Ironically, my father and my mother were born and raised on two islands no more than thirty miles apart, yet they didn't meet until they ventured to New York. What's more, had they met in their home country, their class differences may have kept them from ever marrying.

"My father's parents worked very hard to make ends meet. Daddy, too, had to work hard to help his mother and father maintain their family. Among his chores, as a small boy, was chopping wood for the cookfire and to heat their house early in the morning. After he completed this lengthy task, he walked miles to school, only to invariably get there late. Tardiness was a punishable offense in that day. His teacher frequently laid the whip to him.

"Tired of being beaten, he opted to play hooky at a golden beach by the Caribbean Sea. There, with 3,200-foot-high Nevis Peak behind him, my father would gaze across the horizon and dream of sailing off to his fortune.

"When he was sixteen, my father finally left permanently, stowing away in the hold of a ship. He ended up in the Cuban jungle with several other stowaways who had also come ashore. According to him, they lived there like cavemen, feeding on bananas, coconuts and wild animals. Somehow he learned Spanish. From Cuba, he stowed away on other merchant vessels bound for far-flung ports of the world. He told me he had eventually traveled to South America, to England, and even Germany, during the First World War. But he was most proud that he had been to Africa. He talked about the beauty of the African women. He marveled that they could have many, many children, and yet their breasts stayed filled to beautiful form. 'What a lovely continent,' he said. 'It was just like a paradise.'

"I can still remember how impressed I was at hearing my father chat in some of the six or seven languages he learned during his extensive voyages. Most of the time he would utter a few foreign phrases, then translate what he had said into English. I'd ask him afterward, 'Daddy, how do you know all those languages?' He'd say, 'I had to learn them to survive. You can't be in these countries and not know the language.' He was very proud of being a practical man.

"After World War I broke out, my father could have joined either the American Army or the British Army. He decided upon the British. He was young at the time, and I guess he had some nationalist feelings for his colony's home country. My father hadn't gotten any farther than what we would consider an eighth grade education. He wasn't aware of Britain's imperialistic history. Had he known more about how the Empire felt about Blacks, I don't think he would have been as eager to fight for it. In fact, after the Great War, when the Empire actually acquired new territories in Asia, Africa, and the Pacific because of its military might—strengthened by foot soldiers just like Daddy—my father rued the day he made that choice. The British Army regiment with which he fought, as well as others in France, Belgium, Gallipoli and Palestine, was segregated into all-Black regiments.

"It was in England where my father saw a piano for the first time. He was in a pub when he confronted the mechanical novelty. From the moment he touched the musical instrument, he began to master it. I remember my father playing lovely music on our piano, even though he never had a lesson.

"But he had few such pleasant memories of England. He was forever angry with Great Britain or, as he called it, 'John Bull, the racist.' When the First World War was over and Daddy was discharged, he applied to come to America, but couldn't get a visa. So he stowed away on a ship again. He had heard that America was the land of opportunities and, as he said, he planned to find them.

"Of course, the Immigration and Naturalization Service was very, very strict. They went out and investigated the places where illegal aliens were likely to work and live. At least two or three times they found him, and he was deported back to his country.

"But he always returned, and, finally, the United States immigration officials granted my father some sort of amnesty to remain. Apparently, though his writing skills were poor, he was able to fill out an alien registration card. In America, once a year, they would record an alien registration card for him at the post office.

"He never really wanted to become an American citizen because he was so disappointed in America. 'You know, when I came to this country, I thought the streets of New York were paved with gold.' Both he and my mother had heard wonderful stories in the islands. They had big dreams of coming to America. When they came to America, however, they were able to find shelter only in Black ghettoes. They still had to cope with poverty, lack of opportunity, lack of employment, and racism: all the things that they were running away from in their hope for a better life.

"My father finally acquired a job at Consolidated Edison, the New York City area's electricity and natural gas utility company. He worked in a plant where they made natural gas. He used to get very sick from it and have stomach cramps. Eventually they gave him a position in maintenance. For over thirty years he held that job. He worked at the Courtland Avenue site. I remember it well because many times my father would send me to get his pay envelope. They used to get paid in cash.

"Times were really hard for my parents then. Daddy made about forty, maybe fifty dollars a week. And the rent was fifty dollars a month. Then there was the Con Edison light bill, and other expenses. Even though I was the only child, I understood it was very difficult to make ends meet. I was not showered with a lot of material things. But I was showered with a great deal of love and the knowledge my parents gave me of my heritage and Harlem's. I had just one coat that had to do for school, church on Sunday, and everything else.

"I had one special blue dress that I wore to Sunday school. My mother was Catholic, and she attended St. Mark's Catholic Church here in Harlem. She'd take me with her when she'd go to Mass. My father said that he wasn't getting involved with any religion because he felt that, as a man of African descent, he was a Muslim, who had been robbed of his religion. He never attended any church regularly. The only time he would go was when they had a banquet, and when I was christened at Mother Zion. But that was the limit of his involvement.

"Yet he was knowledgeable about the Bible. And he had a great deal of faith in God which he passed on to me.

"Although my father ran away to America, my mother came to the United States because she was to live with her Aunt Louisa. Aunt Louisa had married a Jewish man in America and was living in very comfortable circumstances. So she sent for Momma. Momma's half-sister Camily was also living in New York.

"Momma was quite beautiful, but she was also sort of wild. I say that she had a lot of heart. She just did what she wanted to. She wasn't the kind of woman you could contain, and she just didn't go along with things because everybody else did them.

"She also liked the good life. My aunt Camily would say to her, 'Alfrieda, let me put your money away.' She said my mother was a spendthrift who would insist on buying the most fabulous, beaded dresses of the time. She would wear an outfit once and then not want to wear it anymore. Years later my aunt told me, 'Rita, she had such beautiful things that I used to go and get those dresses, and I'd hang them outside on my clothesline. I wanted my neighbors to feel that I was wearing all these beautiful clothes, even her underwear.'

"Aunt Camily said to me, 'Your mother was a white woman, and that was it.' What she meant was that because Momma had been spoiled with material things all of her life—a claim which few black girls back then could make—she had the luxury of developing the vanity and independence that was more characteristic of a pampered white woman. She was something!

"At one point she did her little show biz thing. She danced at the Cotton Club. And she went to speakeasies. At one of them she met my father.

"My father, who had never had much joy in life, must have been intoxicated by my mother's fiery spirit and fun loving nature. He spent all he had taking her to nice places.

"Not long afterward they got married. First, they lived down in the predominantly Black neighborhood known as San Juan Hill, in the West Sixty streets. Later that area became the location for the stage play and movie, *West Side Story*. Today it's where the marvelous Lincoln Center complex has been built and has gentrified the entire Upper West Side. But, back then, San Juan Hill was a crowded bunch of ramshackle apartments, saloons, brothels and muddy streets.

"They had an apartment on the top floor of an apartment building. My mother loved everything to look nice and beautiful, so she decorated the place with taste and color, but little money.

"In the early days of their marriage she liked to throw parties and entertain at dinner parties. The famous drummer and bandleader Chick Webb, who introduced singer Ella Fitzgerald to the world, was one of my parents' associates. The whole scene, the kind of people that were interesting in the Harlem community, brought out my mother's lively nature. Perhaps that was why she attracted my father.

"For a short while, both my parents loved the high times, parties, and liquor. Momma was very popular. She believed in letting the good times roll. When she felt good, like when she heard hot music at a block party, she liked to dance. She'd get out there and shimmy like when she was at the Cotton Club. But, not long after they moved to Harlem,

34

my father started to get seriously involved in the regular meetings that were held at the Liberty Hall on West 135th Street—where the black nationalists met and talked about the problems of black people in New York and the world.

"At this point in their marriage, Momma's and Daddy's interests were becoming sharply divided. His focus was now on black nationalism. My mother was less political. She talked about the dominant culture, about European and American values, about Bartholomew Dias, the Portuguese and all of our relatives. Their increasing arguments made our home life chaotic, although I was too young to compare it with much else. Yet, in retrospect, my parents exposed me to a wide breadth of the outside world; not only colorful stories from history and important events, but also everyday gossip and working class dreams about life in New York City as we knew it."

2

The Anger of My Father

On this particular August evening, Rita had been at Well's Eatery outlining her plans to revitalize the burned out buildings on West 143rd Street over chicken and waffles, a Harlem delicacy, with a senior citizen, Mrs. Andrews, whom Rita had met at the Fred Samuel's Political Club. At seventy, Mrs. Andrews' black wig was swept back in an exotic bun which reflected a vitality belying her years. Despite the age difference between the two women, a strong comraderie had developed.

They were still talking animately on the drive back to

the Rangel Development where Mrs. Andrews lived,
when another issue distracted Rita.

"Would you mind if we stopped by my apartment for
a few minutes, Mrs. Andrews? I just want to check that
my kids are safely home."

"Not at all, dear," Mrs. Andrews said, frowning and
adjusting her glasses. "It's tough raising kids right in
these times."

Rita nodded, her genial mood clouding over for a
moment. It was more than tough; it was damned near
impossible. There was not an inch of space along these
streets where your child was not in danger—of con-
tracting disease, of being abused, of being trapped into
taking or selling drugs.

She made her usual smooth turn from Lenox onto
143rd Street and consoled herself. At least she had al-
ready made some progress in renovating the building in
which they lived. The upper part had been repainted a
rich coffee brown, trimmed with beige, and the rest
refaced in brick. A stone planter stood in front. She
smiled to herself, her parents would have been so proud
of her, she thought, looking around. Admiring the sight
for a moment, Rita slowed the car and then began to
pull into an empty space at the curb.

"*I* was really a daddy's girl. Even today, if I close my eyes,
I can conjure a living color picture of myself as a little girl,
walking down 143rd Street, my father holding my hand.

"To me, my father is very tall. As we walk, I look at all
the apartment buildings, their stoops peppered with neighbors. Daddy's very proud of me, and when he stops occasionally to talk to a neighbor, Mrs. Francis for instance, and

she asks how I'm doing, he announces, 'Very well, Mrs. Francis. Rita's a smart girl.' That was a very special time for me. My mother worked during the day, and Daddy took care of me.

"My father, 'Webbie' everybody called him, was a man with a strong presence—six-foot-one, jet black skin, a broad, flat nose, and a jutting forehead. He watched the world through narrowed eyes, and met the world (and the pretty women of whom he was fond) with a well-tended head of hair which he slicked down with hair tonic so that the waves formed a soft, sensual pattern. Daddy was well dressed. His shoes always shined, and he was a vision of dignity when he strode tall and straight on a Harlem street.

"He would stand on the corner by the lamp post across the street from our apartment, smoking his Havana cigar, talking politics and problems of the world with the guys on the block. That was how people socialized in our neighborhood. A good pool player, Daddy occasionally went up to the poolroom on 145th Street to match his skills against the local competition. Other times he'd take me to 144th Street to visit his friend George Isaacs. The neighborhood was his life. It was where he'd walk up and down familiar byways, meeting acquaintances, talking about hopes and dreams, asking, 'Hey, have you heard any news from St. Kitts?'

"Momma and Daddy made lots of friends in those days at the Caribbean social clubs. Every nation in the West Indies, Montserrat and St. Kitts had clubs in Harlem, where transplants would get acquainted with their countrymen and women. The clubs would give dances and invite other West Indians so that there was a large group of Islanders in the community who knew each other.

"These friends became like family to us. Leah and Vita

were closer to Momma than some of her own family who lived right in town, but to whom she hadn't spoken in more than twenty years. Those women would be made up so well that they rivaled the theatrical women in appearance. When Momma would go to their houses, she would always take me along because I was, as she proudly put it, her 'lights, liver and lungs.' She would beam, boasting of my good grades and my ready mind.

"But Momma wasn't any good with economics. She couldn't get us through a week with groceries, regardless of how much money she started with. She lived big for one or two days, but before long, since she didn't know how to budget, she was telling my father, 'Webbie, we need . . .'

"Also, Momma had begun playing the numbers—the illegal neighborhood lottery—with money my father gave her. Once, instead of telling my father where the money had gone, she kept it mum . . . until he happened to walk by the landlord agent's office one day. Mr. McNofsky, the agent, said, 'Mr. Webb! Can you come in for a minute?' Daddy said, 'Well, yes.' Mr. McNofsky told him, 'Mr. Webb, you haven't paid your rent for two months. Is there anything wrong?' My father was flabbergasted. When he got home, he and my mother lit up the house with sparks for two days. 'Freida, what's wrong with you? I give you money, and you don't pay rent.'

"After a while, she'd miss paying our utility bill too. This was especially bad since my father worked for the utility company. 'What are you trying to do, Freida? Trying to get me fired? You know I work at this company, so you've got to pay the bill,' I remember him saying one time. 'They call me into the office at work and ask me, "Webb, what seems to be the trouble in your paying?"

"It soon became apparent that Momma had a serious weakness for the numbers. Daddy constantly told her, 'The numbers is all you live for.' When any particular number would hit, she could tell you the last day, month and year it had hit. Each morning she'd sit down at the table with her pencil and paper and do what she'd call 'dope' out her formula for the number she eventually played that day. Part of the ritual included reading the *Daily News*. There, by examining the comic strip 'Ching Chow,' she'd either spot or imagine numbers in the picture where nobody else saw anything. Later in the day, she'd lean out the window of our apartment and spot passersby. She'd get their attention, 'Ps-s-st! Hey! What was the number?' By day's end, she knew all the results of the horse races at Belmont, Aqueduct and Brooklyn, the daily numbers being dependent on the order in which the horses finished.

"While Daddy kept me enthralled with his stories about great African kings and queens and historical tales that were unheard of at the time, Momma would play her numbers. They grew more estranged. Daddy talked to me about the great universities such as the one at Timbuktu that black people had organized. He told me that Columbus hadn't really discovered America, that black people had come over to the Western Hemisphere first and had shown him the route. In a thousand different ways, he told me how beautiful, how great the African people were.

"All the wonderful things my father talked about sounded like part of some big fantasy. Few black people talked like that during the 1940s and 1950s. His was like a voice in the wilderness. Yet today the very same things that my father told me about are accepted. So he gave me a very, very good concept of myself. I felt connected to a great history. And I was very proud to be what I was.

"In spite of his pride, my father was very bitter. He was just as hostile towards the white world as he was zealous about pan-Africanism. He felt whites had taken all of our history from us. He resented the writers of European and American history for pretending that accomplishments like the consolidation of the vast Songhay kingdom or the accumulation of treasures by the Mali empire had never happened.

"He told me how badly he was treated in New York when he first arrived. He said you couldn't even ride the trolley car along 145th Street because the Irish lived in Harlem at the time, and they would beat you up. Blacks weren't wanted on buses. But the Caribbeans who moved here weren't taking those beatings meekly. They fought back.

"Daddy told me that, until 1930, Harlem Hospital, though it was right in the heart of the black community, had been completely staffed by white doctors and nurses. It took young Adam Clayton Powell, Jr., a minister's son, to organize citizens and black medical professionals to demand the right to work there. He told me about Powell's 'Don't Buy Where You Can't Work' boycotts in 1937 that integrated the staffs of department stores on 125th Street where blacks poured out their money as loyal customers, but where they couldn't work except as menials. Powell marshalled city bus boycotts until Samuel Howell became the first black bus driver ever hired in New York City, with more drivers and mechanics to follow him.

"Daddy talked about all the contradictions in America. And the 'Jim Crowism.' Just as he had sarcastically referred to Great Britain as 'John Bull, the racist,' he used the term, 'Jim Crow,' as did other blacks back then, to refer to American discrimination. At that time there was a popular song called 'Praise the Lord, and Pass the Ammunition.' My father didn't even want to hear that. He preferred the words, 'Praise the Lord, and stop the Jim Crowism.'

"Prior to the marches led by Martin Luther King, prior to anyone ever hearing about Malcolm X, Daddy told me about the racial terrorism going on in the southern states. Since my father couldn't read, he learned about the lynchings from the radio and from weekly meetings with his nationalist group, the Universal Negro Improvement Association. This group was organized by Marcus Garvey in his homeland of Jamaica. In 1918, Garvey started a branch in Harlem, which became his headquarters. And my father, hearing Garvey speak, became an avid follower of his. In fact, it seemed as if Daddy had found a purpose in life; he became totally involved in the Back-to-Africa philosophy of Marcus Garvey and black nationalism. And he lived it day and night.

"In all his travels to Europe, Africa, the Caribbean, and in the States, Daddy had seen that Blacks were never in control of their destinies, but were instead exploited and subjected to oppressive treatment. He had internalized his father's resentment about being a slave. He had watched the tons of raw materials being loaded onto the docks of the Caribbean Islands bound for European and American factories. And Daddy was learning at these nationalist forums how New Yorkers and other people in power had institutionalized racism by writing them into the law books. It was these observations that led him to get involved with Marcus Garvey.

43

"Garvey had built the UNIA into the world's most powerful black group. At its peak during the 1920s, the UNIA amassed an estimated six million members in nine hundred branches internationally. By the twenties, Garvey was every bit as popular among blacks as Booker T. Washington had been at the turn of the century, although Garvey was perceived to be much more of a threat to the white establishment. Washington believed that blacks should become economically necessary to whites by excelling in manual trades such as brickmasonry, carpentry and farming. He did not think rocking the boat for integration would win acceptance. In 1895, Washington told white businessmen, 'In all things that are purely social, we can be as separate as the fingers, yet one as the hand in all things essential to mutual progress.'

"Garvey, however, felt differently. He came along in the years following the First World War—the war in which blacks like my father had fought under the Union Jack, or under the Star and Stripes, thinking that their valor for their countries would finally earn them inclusion. They were wrong. Garvey pointed out the glaring inequities in society. 'Up you mighty race! You can accomplish what you will!' was Garvey's rallying cry.

"Furthermore, in a time when manufacturers were crying for cheap, black labor to man the turbines of mass production, Garvey was preaching that blacks should work for themselves by setting up their own enterprises. He backed up what he preached, too. The UNIA and its Negro Factories Corporation operated myriad enterprises: three grocery stores, a bakery on Seventh Avenue, a laundry/dressmaker/tailor shop on West 142nd, a millinery shop, a restaurant, and a printing press. Of course, Garvey is best known as the proponent of the Back to Africa movement, a campaign in which he encouraged millions of African Americans to repatriate to Liberia. His trans-Atlantic shipping line, Black Star Lines, was to transport these masses.

"But the establishment pegged him a dangerous demagogue, and the FBI built a case against him on charges that he defrauded his members through the mails. My father said the reason the government was able to make a case against Garvey was that some of his own followers had betrayed him and turned him in out of jealousy.

"Even after he was arrested, imprisoned and exiled to Jamaica, Garvey's followers—Garveyites as they came to be known—met each week on 135th Street. On Speakers Corner, where Garvey won over the citizens of Harlem with his soapbox oratory, and his zeal, Garveyites gave speeches on the sidewalk in front of the school, discussing racism and what we as a people had to do to make life better for ourselves today.

Because of his overwhelming respect for Garvey, everything in my father's life eventually became a function to prove Garvey a prophet. 'You know, Marcus Garvey said this,' and 'Marcus Garvey believes that,' peppered his speech.

"As well as going to see Garvey, Daddy would faithfully attend other lectures, for instance in the present Schomburg Center for Research in Black Culture, a repository for the largest collection of books and papers on black people in the world.

"That's where my father learned about Emmett Till. In the summer of 1955, Till, a fourteen year old Chicago boy, went to visit relatives in the town of Money, Mississippi. One day, as he passed a young white woman on the street,

Till was said to have whistled at her and to have looked upon her with something other than deference. In fact, he is said to have engaged in what Southerners called 'reckless eyeballing.' Several white men decided that the penalty for Till's alleged transgression was to be death. They kidnapped the teenager, tortured, castrated, and murdered him, then tossed his body into a nearby river. After it was recovered, photographer Moneeta Sleet of Jet Magazine took shocking pictures of the boy's mutilated body which proved the brutality that modern lynchings still inflicted on black men. Black Americans were enraged. Daddy was one of them.

"Till's was just another in a needless series of southern lynchings. Many occurred because white women claimed they were raped by black men. My father frustratedly said, 'A lot of that rape stuff is not really true. A lot of them white women wanted to be involved with those black men, but when they got caught they claimed they were raped.'

"My father was also frustrated because of his own limitations. For one thing, he was not able to read. And he was frustrated in resolving the overwhelming consequences of poverty and racism that were affecting his life. Of course, he grew bitter. Awful things had happened to him and continued to happen to him.

"As time went on, my father became almost fanatical about injustice against black people in America. In his island-tinged, British accent, he said, 'Rita, we're not going to make it here. You got to do like Garvey said. You got to go back to Africa.'

"If my mother was nearby and heard him, however, she'd fire back, 'Well, David, when you go back, you're going by yourself. 'Cause I surely ain't goin' wich you.' She always used to say, 'When black folks get power, they just can't handle it. We're not ready. You can talk all that black stuff you want, but anywhere there's a whole lot of Negroes, you won't find me.' Meanwhile, Momma was living on 143rd Street in the biggest black community in America.

"Momma had her own concept of black history. Oh, she acknowledged that black kings in antiquity had indeed ruled over great civilizations. But she hypothesized that they had fallen, not because of invasion by outside hordes, but because Africans were inherently cruel and couldn't get along with each other.

"She'd remind Daddy that when they came to Harlem, they had invested in a black business. They'd bought shares in an investment for the refurbishing of the Renaissance Theater on Seventh Avenue. The venture never repaid them their money.

"At a time in American political history when Joseph McCarthy was running around finding Communists, Momma also scolded my father that his conversation could have been construed as un-American. She told him that he'd better be careful or else he could be arrested for communist sympathies. 'Why don't you stop that? You're just making yourself sick.'

"In fact, my father did develop hypertension. Whether it was heredity, consequences of overwork on a poor diet, or the intensity of his feelings, he had a stroke in the early 1950s and developed pleurisy. When he became seriously ill, his employer, Con Edison, used to send doctors to our house almost everyday to treat him and to take his blood pressure.

"Despite his illness, he still continued going to meetings and having fierce discussions about his people. He hated seeing African Americans denying what we were, de-

47

nying our history, ultimately denying our very right to live. And my father recognized this in our friends and neighbors all the time. That's why calling attention to blacks' inferiority complex conditioning and railing against racism became his total life.

"Daddy addressed our people as "black" while others were still calling them Negroes and long before most of us had conceded that black was beautiful. Because of his outspoken opinions some people resented him. They'd tell my mother, 'I want your husband to stop calling me black. I'm colored.' If Momma chastised him because of her friends' complaints, he'd say to them, 'What's wrong with you? Can't you see you're black? You're so ignorant!'

"Every time I had a birthday, my godmother Leah brought me a big, white doll with blond hair. Even if Daddy wasn't around when she gave me the doll, when he returned home, he'd automatically come through the door and say, 'Now, where is it? Where is it?' He'd find it in my bedroom. And right in the garbage can it would go. I used to stare bewilderedly at my father while he went through this entire ritual over a piece of hard plastic covered in doll clothes.

"But one thing about Daddy, if he threw it away, he replaced it. He'd announce, 'Tomorrow, we're going to Blumstein's.' Blumstein's was the biggest department store in Harlem, a major attraction for shopping on 125th Street. My father would march me in there and proudly pick out a black doll for me. He'd point to its face, with that blank stare that dolls have, and proclaim to me, 'This is you. This is what you're about.' This was supposed to be a compliment. It never occurred to Daddy that I might not have liked being told I was an inanimate toy. 'You saw how much this doll cost, didn't you? What does that tell you?'

"At that point, Daddy may have been psychotic in his fanaticism. You could never have an ordinary conversation with him without his going off on a tangent about race. But at least he was providing me with his world view.

"As my father said, 'The only time The Man can enslave you is when you're not knowledgeable about the system.' Daddy would preach, 'If you don't know the language of the oppressor, you'll always be enslaved. You have to be educated, you have to know how to negotiate and move that system for the betterment of yourself, of your neighbors, of your people. The only time he can box you in is when you can't go beyond the corner of the street you live on because you're too fearful of what's out there.'

"So, as you can imagine, as my Daddy's girl, school was an important rite of passage for me. First, I went to an elementary school named after Countee Cullen, a beloved black poet of the Harlem Renaissance who wrote the poem, *What is Africa to Me?* Cullen's widow faithfully came to make a speech every year.

"I found learning fascinating, especially learning about democracy, and its checks and balances. Civics and citizenship classes made me realize even more that—even though I was black, even though I didn't have all the money in the world—I didn't need to feel locked in. I learned that if I didn't get any answers on one level, I could go to the next level and the next level, until I got answers, until I was able to change things. With that knowledge, I always felt very free. I went to a school in my neighborhood, so I had never actually had any involvement with white kids. In the sixth grade there was an exchange program which brought kids from a white school to meet with us and which took us to visit them. Most black kids never dealt with white kids unless they chose high schools with certain rigid academic courses of study. Julia Richman, Washington Irving, and Hunter were all Manhattan high schools with high academic achievement requirements.

"Still, I never felt that I had been left out of anything. When I attended Julia Richman High School, I was in one of the top classes. I felt that I could compete just as well as anyone, so I didn't feel any different.

"During those days, I remember my family really struggling. The Valley area of Harlem was known as a poverty pocket where all the poor people remained. It was overcrowded; people had chintzy salaries; they did menial jobs. Our house was very basic—nothing fancy, except my mother's good taste.

"Whenever it was time for me to get new shoes, my mother would take me to the shoe shop run by a Greek man on 144th Street and Lenox. My mother, in passing (and in preparing him to be generous with his credit) would tell him, 'Rita needs a pair of new shoes.' So he would say, 'Bring her in. Let's fit her for some shoes. I'll fix them up, put a heel on them, and shine 'em up.' What he was actually doing was repairing a pair of shoes that someone else had left. But, despite their hand-me-down background, I would be so very happy for those shoes.

"One time I'll never forget was in either second or third grade. My mother had taken me to buy a pair of new sneakers. Apparently she couldn't find any in my size for the right price. She ended up buying sneakers that were so big they would just shake in the front. And I felt so embarrassed when I wore them, but I just pretended that everything was all right. Then I got in a very embarrassing position at school. My teacher took my class out for recreation in the yard at Countee Cullen School, Public School 194, and we were playing "The Farmer in the Dell," the child's game where you had to skip around. When it came time for me to skip, the whole front end and toe section of these too-large sneakers just waggled. Everybody in the class was staring, but I just acted like there was nothing strange about me. 'The farmer in the dell, the farmer in the dell, hi, ho, the merry-oh, the farmer in the dell.' Wouldn't this song ever end? I tried skipping faster. That only sped up my flip-flopping shoes so they were just like jackhammers slapping the blacktop, 'Wapp-a-pap! Wapp-a-pap!' A full beat after I'd skipped a step. The kids started laughing.

"I tried to disregard a whole yard of my classmates— my peers pointing their fingers at my feet and forcing their voices into that high-pitched, nagging, 'you're so stupid' laugh. But, at some point, I gave up the charade. When I sheepishly glanced at some of their devilishly excited eyes, and they saw my vulnerability, that's when they really bored in on me. By the time I had finished skipping my turn, I was so embarrassed that all I could do was avoid their eyes. Hanging my head down, I stared with flush-faced anger at those disgusting, flip-floppy shoes my mother had bought me. I hated being poor.

"But, regardless of how bad things were, we never let other people know. That's the way my mother and father operated. If we didn't have anything to eat, we got some tea, or some water and sugar, drank it so that we'd have something in our stomachs, wiped our faces, and acted like everything was wonderful. No one was supposed to know.

"After elementary school, at Julia Richman High

School, I was always in a college bound class. No vocational class tracking for me. I had made up my mind I wasn't growing up to do housework; I was on my way to a higher education. By the time I graduated from junior high, for instance, I had already had three years of French language.

"I took French because I had a cousin, Ruby, who lived in Paris. She was a dancer at the Folies Bergere under the name ZZ Richards, with the Richards pronounced in the French manner. Ruby was Aunt Camily's daughter. Like Josephine Baker, Ruby had gone to France because there were greater opportunities for black entertainers to be headliners at the big clubs than in America. There were also lots of French speakers in my neighborhood; persons from Dominica, and Guadaloupe, and Martinique.

"Times were still hard. There were days when the only reason I was able to get to school was because I had a bus pass. I would leave in the morning, and my mother would say, 'Listen, I'm going to see what I can do. Maybe by the time you come home I can borrow some money from somebody.' There were lunch specials which only cost thirty-five cents. Soup and a sandwich cost twenty-five cents. Yet, some days I didn't even have money for that. That's how life was.

"When my friends would ask me, 'Are you coming with us to the cafeteria?' I'd say, 'Oh, no. I'm going to Chock Full 'O' Nuts down on 67th Street and have lunch there.'

"Actually, I would go into the girls' bathroom for the whole forty-five minute period. I'd stand in there and look like I was washing up. In between other girls' visits there, I'd dream about one day having a refrigerator full of food in my own home.

"When I'd see my girlfriends after lunch, and they'd ask me how my lunch was, I'd say, 'It was just great. I had . . .' No one ever knew that I was really hungry. Because that was the way I was raised. As soon as the dismissal bell jangled the school hallways, I would dash home to eat dinner. But sometimes the only thing we could afford were french fries, because potatoes were only five cents a pound. Other times we'd have to eat something called a johnnycake, plain bread fried in a pan, with a little sugar sprinkled on it. We ate it and made out the best we could.

"I endured hardships growing up and learned how to maintain a front. Going through those difficulties and trying to keep the strength to maintain were hard. But I kept on going to school because I figured that once I got an education, it couldn't be taken from me. And with that bus pass in hand, I made it everyday.

"Early on, I realized that my father had a girlfriend who lived up the block in Number 139. A woman by the name of Miss Johnson. Sometimes, when he would baby-sit me, he would take me to her house. Nothing ever occurred in front of me; I don't even think anybody ever told me, but I just knew that she was his girlfriend.

"One time this adulterous affair kept my mother up all night. I first noticed when, at about ten o'clock—a time when she was usually long since in bed—she was pacing by the window. 'I'm tired of this,' I heard her murmur to herself, a slow burn detectable in the words that she bit off. I said, 'Mommie, what's wrong?' She was crying about my father hanging out with Miss Johnson. I was a little girl, but

Momma had nobody to talk to but me. 'Momma, don't cry,' I said. 'We can just get another daddy.'

"For most of the night I, too, looked out the window. I kept my sights trained up the block toward Number 139 because I knew Daddy would be coming from there. Back in those days, men often wore very sporty, two-tone spectator shoes. When dawn broke, I spotted my father stepping out from Miss Johnson's apartment building, wearing his brown-and-white spectators. I said, 'He's coming now, Momma! He's coming now!' And my mother was sort of relieved.

"But Daddy was still a player. That hurt my mother, and their relationship further deteriorated over the years. Finally, she lost affection for him and started sleeping in a room by herself. I used to hear them arguing, and then her saying, 'Just don't touch me.' Momma wasn't happy, and she continued on until she was very, very bitter. My mother was a typical West Indian woman of her time. Most of them believed that it was better to have a man, even a playboy, than to be alone. And they'd put up with a beau or husband even if he was having children by another woman. So, even though my mother often threatened to leave, she never did. Part of the reason was that she needed Daddy for his meager income. It was sad, because I wanted my parents to be together. When they argued, there'd be a lot of tension in the house, and then I'd be unhappy. I said in my mind that I didn't want to ever live like that. I would try to look for other ways to resolve problems and negotiate around them.

"When my mother would get angry, even if it wasn't with me, she would say, 'I'm just going to put you in an orphanage, Rita.' She had described these orphanages to me—about how terrible they were and how the waifs had to get up at five o'clock in the morning to scrub floors, and how that kind of stoop labor had deformed their backs. And I could just imagine the heavy wooden door being locked behind me as I was admitted to one of these horror houses. I'd plead, 'Oh, Mommie, please, you and Daddy try to work this out.'

"On the other hand, my father would say, 'If it wasn't for you, Rita, I would not stay here.' I sadly realized my parents were hanging in because I was in the picture, but neither was really doing what they wanted to do.

"So, I was always insecure because if the two of them really did reach their limit with each other, I didn't know what was going to happen to me. I saw all of these serious things happening, and, consequently, I became a very serious child. And I couldn't grow up fast enough. I was just trying to hang in until I could grow up and take care of myself. I think I learned very early to assume responsibility for those people who are vulnerable because I know how vulnerable I myself felt.

"It was during this time my father grew more ill, however, and I had to take time out from school to take care of him. My mother wasn't going to do it. She said that he had done a lot of mean things to her, and that she wasn't going to knock herself out. She didn't care.

"The main thing she cared about at that point was that he got to work and brought home that pay envelope. That hurt me, so I took the responsibility. I wanted so much for him to live, and was so happy when he saw me graduate.

"Daddy's hypertension worsened. He started getting severe headaches. The doctor at Con Edison told him to lay off pork, salty foods or alcohol. But my father liked his pork, his salty codfish, and his rum or scotch. In addition, he liked to smoke Havana cigars, and he wasn't about to give up his few pleasures.

"One winter's day in 1955, several months after the Till lynching, Daddy was standing on the street by his favorite lamppost. He was supposed to be on bedrest. Instead, he was smoking his usual Havana and excitedly making his point to some acquaintances about his usual topic. '. . . do you mean to tell me that those crackers down south did this to this black boy, and they're going to get away with it? You New Yorkers take this too lightly. You all need to be marching.'

"Then, all of a sudden, Daddy's eyes bulged for a moment and closed. He dropped to the ground where his head banged against the pavement. Men swarmed around to revive him. The commotion down on the street outside the River's Edge Bar caught Momma's attention as she happened to lean from her window perch. 'Mrs. Webb,' one of the men shouted up when he saw her, 'Mrs. Webb, your husband just fell down. Come right now!'

"When she reached him, my mother comforted Daddy. 'Be calm, Webbie. You're going to be all right.' Finally the ambulance arrived. At Harlem Hospital, the emergency room was overworked and overcrowded. Doctors and nurses whisked through on their way to new crises. Meanwhile, incoming patients were being put on gurneys in the hallways because there weren't enough beds. Daddy, by now, was his cantankerous self. 'I'm supposed to have a room!' he bellowed to my mother, purposely loud enough to be heard by everyone within yards around. An unsus-

56

pecting nurse passed by. 'Nurse!' he commanded, 'I demand a room right now!'

"It worked. He was finally given a room where he and my mother waited until a doctor could come in and examine him. The doctor, a white man, asked my father to remove his shirt. 'Don't come near me! I don't want no white doctors touching me,' Daddy ordered. 'He's not listening to anything I say,' the doctor told the supervisor.

"For the whole time he was there, my father told everyone that he wasn't going to take medication from, or cooperate with, anyone who wasn't the right color. Finally, after a few days, my mother decided to bring Daddy home A.M.A. (against medical advice). He stayed home for a week or so, then began to get sicker. He couldn't keep food down. He began hallucinating about a visit he'd taken to Philadelphia years ago as a youth. When the Con Edison doctor visited him, he ordered Daddy back to the hospital. Daddy listened.

"But, soon, he was demanding to be brought back home again; so the doctors ordered the nurse to strap him to the bed. On my final visit to see him, Daddy told me that his roommate had allowed the hospital officials to do this to him when he should have been standing up and protesting against their treatment of black men. I looked over at the man in the other bed. The man was comatose. Later I learned that the man hadn't been conscious since before my father was brought there.

"On January 26, 1956, my father died.

"I guess you could say that the pain of racism finally killed Daddy; he had suffered his second and fatal stroke while arguing over what black folks should do about Emmett Till's lynching.

"Instead of classifying his death as attributable to hypertension, however, the coroner said that my father's death was suspicious because of the wound on his skull. They refused to allow us to take the body to a funeral home. Instead, the body was taken to the city's Bellevue Hospital where the medical examiner conducted a full investigation. My mother was brought in for questioning. She managed to convince him that the wound had occurred from Daddy's hitting his head on the pavement, and afterward we were allowed to take the body.

"But then Momma almost caused my Daddy's still body to turn a somersault—she refused to take him to any black undertaker in Harlem. Instead, she took my father's corpse to Walter B. Cooke, a white mortician on East 86th Street, because she didn't want any of our West Indian friends trying to get lucky by hiding notes to the dead in the coffin. In Caribbean culture, the people still believed in the occult. Some of their deepest beliefs had to do with the dead. Momma didn't want anyone interfering with her husband's departure.

"Then there was the matter of the $5,000 insurance money. The funeral cost something like $2,000 as my mother bought a beautiful casket and grave at Woodlawn Cemetery. After the funeral, however, she must have still continued to splurge with the windfall money. We had a joint account. Yet, when I asked her what she was doing to cause the balance to dwindle down so quickly, she snapped, 'It's none of your business.' She was also entitled to Con Ed's minuscule pension for widows—ten dollars a week after Daddy's thirty years of service. The little money

Momma received ran out very quickly and she was almost destitute except for what I could give her.

"To this day I wince thinking of all those hardworking years Daddy put in and how little reward he or his family received for all his faithful service."

3

Age of Enlightenment

"I'll only be a moment, Mrs. Andrews."

Suddenly, Rita spotted her seven year old twins, Abena and Ayana, on the sidewalk stoop. She was about to yell out a scolding when she noticed her sons, Mark and Peter. They all started running toward the car. Rita's heart began pumping uncontrollably. Before she'd flung the car door open, she knew something terrible had occurred.

Walking toward them, she demanded hoarsely, "What is it? What's happened?"

Abena, the smaller twin, could hardly speak. She was

sobbing uncontrollably. "Momma," she exclaimed between sobs, "David just got shot!"

Rita's heart beat even faster. "Where is he? How did it happen?"

Mark stood speechless, his body trembling.

"What happened?" she repeated softly. "Don't be afraid, Mark. Just tell me all of it."

Mark began to pour out the whole story. "Before the guy could get off another shot, David ran off in one direction, and the guy ran off in the other. At first I didn't know what the hell had happened. When I heard the POW, I knew there'd been a shot or shots fired. But I didn't think David got hit because he ran like hell. A couple of Muslims and I went right back to the shop. We figured David would run maybe a couple of blocks and come back around. So we waited and waited. But it's been about forty-five minutes to an hour, and he still hasn't shown up. We don't know where he is. Maybe you'd better go down to the hospital and see if he's there. It was all my fault," he concluded miserably.

Rita closed her eyes, trying to keep back the tears. She knew that she had to be strong. She knew she couldn't panic. She had to move swiftly, but calmly. She looked into Mark's eyes. "No, it's not your fault. This," she said quietly and made a wide sweeping gesture indicating the atmosphere, "is at fault." She reached out to touch Mark's shoulder to transmit to him and all her children strength and comfort.

Her sixteen year old daughter Gladys popped up. "Mom, I can take care of everyone."

Rita nodded. "Mark, come with me. Gladys, take the

62

kids inside and try to quiet them down. I'm going over to the hospital."

Slowly, but determinedly, she walked back to her car. Turning once to wave to the younger children, she watched them disappear into the building. Safely inside the car, she leaned her head against the cool steering wheel and paused to say a silent prayer. Mrs. Andrews reassured her, "Everything will be all right, Rita." Rita nodded uncertainly.

"*I*n my senior year of high school, a classmate at Julia Richman High School introduced me to a young man from Wrightsville, Georgia, named Theroin Davis. He was almost a decade my senior. Theroin was in the United States Army, but he told me that he would be discharged shortly. Almost at first sight, he expressed a great deal of interest in me, and I was intrigued.

"I wasn't used to men's attention. I hadn't been exposed to many men due to my mother's close chaperoning. In fact, the closest I'd ever come to romance was reading *True Romance* magazine. Growing up, I had my childlike fantasies about love and marriage. I envisioned my future husband as a man with a responsible career: a doctor, lawyer, businessman or government worker. We would live in a beautiful home, with one or two children, wonderful neighbors, and the best that life had to offer. We'd have the kind of life that I had seen the family in the **Dick and Jane Readers** living.

"All during high school I knew I wanted to go on to college. Howard University was my first choice. But my parents had objected to my choice because I'd be away from their day-to-day supervision. They even objected to my going a half-mile away to the Harlem Hospital School of Nursing, knowing I'd be living away from home in the student nurses' dormitory during the week. I began to long to be on my own and in control of my own life.

"Even before Daddy was gone, I began to fantasize about getting married because I saw it as my only alternative to freedom. Theroin Davis became the object of my affections. I remember my first date with him which was, in fact, my first date with a real live man. We went to see a movie at the Loews Theater.

"While sitting in the darkened moviehouse with my date, I began to tremble to the point that I know it was noticeable. I was filled with anxiety. I finally had to contemplate what this man really wanted out of our relationship.

"One night I spoke with him about his expectations of me. I explained to him that I would not consider becoming involved sexually. I explained to him that my mother used to recite to me an old saying, 'If a man can get the milk for free, why buy the cow?'

"In those times, if you had the kind of parents that I did, you went ahead and married, rather than disgrace your family, if your neighbors found out you had either been sexually intimate prior to marriage or that you were having a baby out of wedlock. If the young man involved was unwilling for holy matrimony, the young woman was usually sent away to another state to live with a family member until the baby was born. It was kept a secret from people in the neighborhood. Unfortunately, in some cases the young woman was put out of the home to fend for herself after disgracing the family.

"In those days the major responsibility for maintaining a relationship that was sex-free was placed on the woman.

So, during my courtship with Theroin, whom I would eventually marry, I decided that the best way to avoid getting caught in a bad position would be to make certain that all of our dates were in public places with many people around us.

"Each weekend Theroin would take me out to a movie or some activity. One day, Mrs. Resington, the tailor's wife, asked my mother if my boyfriend and I were sexually active. My mother took serious exception to her question. 'Of course not!' my mother exclaimed. Mrs. Resington joked, 'Don't tell me the poor man is getting a pig in the bag.' With a resounding curse, Momma put her down in her eloquent West Indian accent.

"Six months after meeting Theroin, he gave me an engagement ring. A short while later we married. I felt I would live happily ever after.

"Unfortunately, what followed was seven years of hardship and heartbreak, not wedded bliss. A year and a half after we married, I had my first baby, Judith Elizabeth Davis, whom everyone calls Judy.

"But money was irregular in our house, since Theroin didn't bring home his paychecks, but would instead lose them gambling, partying and carrying on an affair with a woman he kept on the side.

"In addition to my own problems, after my father died my mother was very lonely. She asked me to come back home and stay with her. 'You're the only child I have,' Momma would say. 'You and your husband can live with me.' I didn't move back immediately, but I spent a lot of time talking with my husband about it. Eventually, after Judy was born, Theroin and I did move in with my mother.

Despite all my grandiose plans, I was right back in the apartment on the street where I grew up.

"For about three years, during which I again became pregnant, I put up with Theroin's infidelity and lack of financial support. In 1959, we separated for the first time. But, despite all my marital problems, New York state's divorce laws at that time only allowed for divorce on grounds of adultery, which was a difficult charge to prove. While I wanted to get out of my marriage, I had to wait until the divorce laws were changed to make abandonment grounds for divorce. When that time came, my husband's own brother helped me by serving my husband the papers. My brother-in-law said that I was a nice person, and I deserved an opportunity to be happy.

"With little support money from my husband, I had to work as a waitress, then in a laundry to keep money coming in to feed my children. I felt overwhelmed, and unable to be the person I felt I was meant to be. Finally, in 1961, the burden was made almost unbearable; my mother died.

"Momma had been ailing for over a year. The doctors couldn't seem to determine what she had, but she had completely lost her appetite. They admitted her to the hospital, but, as Momma said, 'They don't give you much attention when you're poor.' So, she kept complaining, but to no avail.

"Finally, Momma said she was so fed up that she was not going to stay there another day. But when she got home, she got weaker and weaker. In spite of her condition, she was stubborn, and she did not tell me there was anything seriously wrong. Finally I saw her growing thin and crying so much that I convinced her to go back to the hospital. By then I had to hold her up to walk. As we left our building, a guy I knew was on drugs came over and helped me get my mother in a taxi.

"This time the doctors kept her in the hospital and ran test after test. All they told us was they weren't sure of what was wrong, but she continued to deteriorate. Not long after they gave her a fluoroscope, she went into a coma.

"At that point, my mother was receiving my father's Social Security check. The coma had come near the end of the month. Her monthly check was due on the third of the following month. Periodically she would become conscious and ask me, 'Rita, is this the third of the month?' I knew she wanted to live long enough that I could get her check and pay the rent.

"But my mother was suffering. It was agonizing for me to go every day and see her hardly alive. I felt that she really wanted to die. Yet she was trying to hold on until that third of the month.

"One day I went to see her, and she looked especially weak, but she came to for a few minutes and asked me, 'Is this the third?' I just couldn't stand seeing her suffering any more. So I lied, 'Yes, Momma, it's the third,' I said softly.

"At that, she closed her eyes. She didn't say any more. That night she died.

"When I returned to the hospital to claim my mother's body, I looked so very young that the doctor said, 'No, you have to get an older person.' I said, 'I'm of age,' to sign papers or whatever, but, in the end, I had to get a lady from my building to go back to the hospital and convince the man that the hospital should release the body to me.

"When my mother passed away, I didn't get any insurance money. Poor folks in those days did take out personal life insurance, but, when things got financially tight, they cashed in their policies. That's what had happened in my family.

"Before going into the hospital, my mother had begged me to see that when she died she wouldn't be buried in a potter's field, the cemetery for the destitute. She didn't want to be remembered, nor did she want me to be remembered, as not having had enough money to tend to this final financial matter. But, on the other hand, my mother had ordered me, 'Don't you ask anybody for money for my funeral. Don't collect anything for me. I don't want anybody to know we didn't have enough to bury me.'

"Figuring out how to buy my mother's coffin and burial plot was therefore quite a challenge. I had been working and had saved maybe three or four hundred dollars. In the interim, between Momma's death and the funeral, a younger cousin of mine, who lived in the more middle class complex called Riverton Apartments, said she knew people in her building who were morticians, and she promised to help me with my problem if I needed her.

"I tried to follow Momma's wishes and bury her without help, but the days were passing, and I was getting more and more anxious. Finally I asked my cousin's aid, and she took me over to Levy and Delaney funeral parlor. He said that he would do whatever he could to help me. The mortician went to the hospital and got the body. Meanwhile, I managed to raise a little money.

"After my mother's funeral, I knew I was really alone. With my marriage already a shambles, I felt particularly isolated with both of my parents dead and no extended family for a support system. I felt that no one understood me, nor cared.

"I knew my neighbors must have been wondering how

I was going to make it, and for a while so did I. But I asked God for help, and gradually I started to help myself. As I looked around for support, I realized there were a few resources available to me on the block where I lived. For one thing, I had a sense of security living there, and amenities such as my childrens' schools and a nearby job. I struggled on.

"But, financially, I couldn't make it work after my husband moved out. In 1962, I started seeking welfare, a necessity when my husband quit paying child support. I was carrying my third son, Peter, when one day an older lady I knew gave me a book on having positive thoughts to get positive outcomes. The book made me feel better. Later, I was so inspired by another book she suggested, Catherine Marshall's *A Man Called Peter*, the story of her husband Peter Marshall, I decided to name my son after him.

"Nevertheless, when it came time to deliver my child, I was all by myself. It was so bad that I had to pay a friend from Brooklyn to come across the river to get the baby and me when it came time for us to leave Harlem Hospital. I began to wonder if anyone ever helped anyone else without a reward.

"Once I came home, I found that neighbors can be very cold to you when they know you're vulnerable. I know what it's like to be ostracized. To have three kids looking toward you for support, to be poor, young and alone.

"Some people I met added to my sense of an uncaring world. 'Why you have all those kids, girl?' Others who hardly knew me would comment, 'Tsk-tsk. Oooh, my God! Look at that girl with all those children. You young people today . . . You'd better get your tubes tied, honey.' Perfect strangers would comment without the slightest hesitation. I didn't answer, but thought to myself, a man who fathers a lot of children, people will pat him on the back and call him a real man, but when a woman bears several children, people make fun of her.

"When you have several children, everything is a major project. To get on the bus, I'd have to individually lift each one of my kids up to the bottom step. The drivers would often get impatient and shout at me, 'C'mon, lady! Hurry up! Why do you have so many kids?' But I always walked tall. Always kept them neat and clean. I'd wash all day and all night to keep them that way. I hung diapers from wall to wall in our apartment and scrubbed toilets constantly.

"When I took the children to the teacher-parent meetings, other parents got in the habit of seeing me come. Pretty soon they started expecting me, and, if I was late, they'd ask each other, 'Where is that girl with the baby on her hip?'

"When I went shopping, I'd tell the butcher to give each one of the kids a little bag. Our favorite meats were chicken backs and breast of lamb. Both of these were only ten cents a pound, so we'd buy ten pounds each. Or we'd get evaporated milk, and I'd add water to it and a little sweetener because I couldn't afford fresh milk. If I had a few extra coins I'd buy chocolate and enrich the milk.

"In those days, everywhere I turned for help seemed to turn me down. While riding a subway train, I saw an advertisement for Community Services Society along the poster rack that read, 'If you need help, call us.' So I did. But when I went there, authorities at the agency suggested that, as such a young single mother (I was in my early twenties) with so many children (three at this time: Judy, David and Mark), I should turn my children over to foster care.

"I was against that idea right from the start. I knew the foster care system was horrendous. And I knew that if I gave up my children, I might not ever see them again. They'd probably be divided up and sent to different foster homes which would make each of them feel very lonely and scared. Most of all, no one could love them like I could.

"Again, I asked God for strength to hang on. I became very spiritual, reading the Bible regularly. In Ecclesiastes I, I read that there's a time and a season for everything. I took that passage to heart, feeling it meant that there would be a better day in my future than I was then experiencing.

"Time passed, and somehow I struggled on. During the early 1960s, my lifelong race pride was reinforced by hearing great leaders such as Malcolm X. And I kept thinking, I'm so sorry that my father is not alive today. Because he had really been right, but he had been so alone. Now all the doors are opening. All those books that were hidden on the shelves, all those chapters that we had never seen, all those great things that we had never been told about, are now being told to others.

"What was different, of course, was that there were courageous, young black leaders who were giving us direction, who were finally standing up to all of the oppression. I heard about Martin Luther King, and how his followers in the South refused to back off from the fight against segregation, even in the face of the bombing murders of four little girls in a church in Birmingham. Oh, I just wanted to be there to march with them.

"By 1964, a flame had been kindled in me, and I

needed to fight back and to stand up for the things that I believed in. But what could I do?

"I looked around my own community. Right in Harlem we had deterioration and black-on-black crime. I saw the lack of love that we had for each other. I saw the apathy. One of the things I came to realize is that we had to find our own solutions to the problems in our lives and in our world. With my new commitment, I decided to make my contribution on my own street. Another tenant in my building, Ethel Edmondson, who lived in Apartment Number 20, had heard a radio advertisement over WLIB-AM that said that the Congress of Racial Equality, one of the best known civil rights groups of the time, would help community people organize themselves to improve their neighborhoods. In December of 1964, we got them to come to 145th Street, and a man named Paul Gaylord, the head organizer, from C.O.R.E. came to speak.

"He wore his hair in the first Afro I had ever seen. I thought it was the most beautiful thing I had ever seen a man wear. All of the women in the building fell in love with him.

"At that point, my husband had disappeared, and I was completely on my own, sole parent to five young children. My third son, Peter, was just an infant. And I was living in the same apartment that my parents had raised me in. Our building had been built in 1905. The exquisite architecture and designs in the building's layouts still showed the elegance of the day.

"But as had happened with most of the lovely buildings in Harlem, the place had been allowed to run down, and the people living in them weren't receiving proper services. Landlords in Harlem had always taken advantage of the people. No heat. No paint jobs. Leaks for days. Not getting services in the black community has been going on forever. But somehow or other the black people continued to accept that cycle—we continued to pay the rent. Black folks have been conditioned to hardship and to obeying. They do what they're supposed to do. And they have a lot of faith.

"Well, I decided things had to improve, and there didn't seem to be anyone in my life or anywhere else who was going to help. So, I began talking to my neighbors and helped start a tenants' association on West 143rd Street by organizing my building first. We elected officers and, since I was at home on public assistance during the days, I was chosen secretary.

"One of my duties as secretary was to monitor the city inspectors when they came to inspect our apartment building. I wrote down their badge numbers and took notes while they made their inspections.

"We began to maintain clean halls and to improve the services delivered in the building. Miss Daisy and Mr. Thurman bought coal for the furnace so that it never ran out. We tried to get someone on each floor to help.

"If some of the tenants were behind in their rents—in order to limit evictions—we organized house parties and sold dinners to help them.

"Children clustered around me as I went from apartment to apartment every Saturday, handing out flyers to people in other buildings on the block to invite them to meetings which would teach them how to develop their own tenants' groups. If we were ever to improve the conditions in which we lived, one of our first tasks was to make the city—and thus the landlords—more accountable to the city building code. To that end, Paul Gaylord taught us about the Speigel Act—the law that allowed the city Department of Welfare, which paid rents for people on public assistance, to withhold those rents from landlords whose buildings had housing code violations. This pressured landlords to fix problems they may not have otherwise bothered with.

"After we organized in my building, we began to complain about the lack of heat and hot water. There were holes in the walls from broken plaster, often caused by water leaks in steam and water pipes. In my apartment, maggots started coming through my bathroom wall because a rat had died up in the ceiling and was decaying there.

"Eventually I made up a flyer, about the landlord of my building. 'The two-legged rat is getting fat off you!' Then I organized a renters' demonstration in front of his apartment building on the Grand Concourse up in the Bronx. He lived in a nice building, and he didn't want his neighbors to see all of us from Harlem picketing outside with signs. Later he tried to evict me on a 'holdover action.' That means that he wanted me out on a reason other than nonpayment of rent, namely for being a nuisance. But when I contacted a reporter, John Apple, who wrote about my plight, the landlord soon had my apartment repaired and painted. Afterwards, all the neighbors said, 'Oh, look. Rita got him to do something. We should have stayed with her and we'd have gotten him to make repairs, too.' It was my first experience with fighting back and seeing some action.

"I began to dream of co-oping all the houses on the block. Of course, it was just a fantasy. I read about people in other areas of the country who had become owners of their own apartments, and I started to think that we could, too. I wanted a co-op that we could all plan together. Because I had come to ask, what is poverty? Maybe just the fact that we don't own anything. When people are owners, they have more ability to control their lives, and they take more of an interest.

"Looking around for answers, I noticed that people reacted in different ways to being poor. I had seen poor people when Theroin had taken me to visit his family in Georgia and the Carolinas. Yet, down South, whatever those folks owned was as clean as a whistle. And whatever they had they would share. If somebody cooked collard greens from her garden one evening, she would share them with her next-door neighbor. That neighbor, in turn, would share her garden's tomatoes or the catfish she or her husband had caught from the river that day. In the communal atmosphere of these neighborhoods, unlike New York, people didn't pass each other in the street without speaking. But apparently when blacks migrated to the urban centers, that had all been lost.

"I envisioned bringing the extended family concept I'd seen in the South to the big cities. I wanted to reintroduce that concept to my people so that we could ultimately survive here.

"Of course, I knew such grand dreams had to begin somewhere small. Then I noticed that we had a number of other young mothers in my building. Each morning, all of us left the house at the same time, taking our young babies to the same neighborhood school.

"To sell my idea, I went around and knocked on the individual mothers' doors in my building. I would begin by saying, 'I've got an idea. Let's all take turns taking our children to school. That'll mean we all don't have to leave every morning at the same time. When it's my turn, I'll take them all to school and somebody else can pick them up in the afternoon.'

"Each time I'd talk with one of my neighbors, I'd encourage her to commit and find out how she could participate based on her schedule. After checking and double checking with the women, I gave everyone their assignments by writing up a schedule for the entire building. Different mothers escorted the children on a weekly basis and, of course, we'd change schedules if a mother had an emergency.

"We called it the mothers' self-help club. That organization worked so well, by sharing responsibility, that we all got more done than we would have if everybody had done the same thing—taking kids to school and care giving—at the same time.

"That next year, 1965, one of the members of the Harlem Organizing Committee gave me a book called *The Fight for Socialism: The Principles and Program of the Workers Party* by Max Schactman. That book influenced me a great deal at that time. Schactman's classic 1946 treatise on Marxism was a primer for political novices that defined the fundamental cogs in our socioeconomic world—workers and labor, and how capitalists profited by exploiting that labor.

"Before I read that book I wondered why there had to be poverty in a great country like America. After reading about socialism, I focused on the capitalist system and its contradictions. I wondered if this system caused the racism and classism and the awful things that happened to us.

What about the competitiveness of one neighbor against the other, and the feeling of inadequacy because one had much more? So I went through a period when I was questioning the very society that I was living in.

"I was still fearful of the future. So I resorted to the one thing that always brought me consolation: prayer. Again I began to rely on my faith in God. It brought me a positive attitude and helped me continue my social effort bringing people into my life like Dorothy Day.

"I first met her at Maryhouse, one of the homes she founded in the East Village, when I needed help feeding my kids.

"Dorothy was a renowned advocate for the poor who started what was called The Catholic Worker movement in the 1930s. She lived among the homeless and the needy in small communes she set up because, 'man (shows) his faith, his love of God, by his love of brother.' Latter-day activists loved Dorothy Day for her straightforward, liberal theology, and for staunchly challenging church conservatives like Francis Cardinal Spellman. In fact, Abbie Hoffman affectionately called Dorothy, 'the first hippie.' Among other intellectuals she influenced were the Berrigan brothers of Pentagon Papers fame, and Cesar Chavez, the farm workers' union organizer.

"She became my friend, almost a second mother to me. Maybe she empathized with me because, although she had never married, she had had a child from a commonlaw marriage before she gave up a life of hobnobbing among the socialist and literary crowds during the 1920s.

"Later, when I wanted to go back to school, Dorothy helped me pay for my kids to attend parochial school, and she helped me with my son David's private school tuition. Dorothy Day was committed to helping me remain in my community and better it rather than leaving as so many others had done. Gradually so was I."

4

Kinship With the Poets

Turning the key in the ignition, Rita started the drive to Harlem Hospital. She drove slowly, her mind whirling as she spun past familiar sights on the passing streets, trying not to anticipate what awaited her.

This was perhaps the most difficult feat, she thought, not to anticipate a fear-filled future. She tried to gather up her courage. There had been other times when she had been terribly afraid, other grueling, frightening obstacles she had to overcome. She tried to take comfort from that knowledge now. She'd made it through bad times before.

"*I*n those early years of my social activism, I moved from remodeling my building, to improving the quality of life on my block. I organized a block association, The Community League of West 143rd Street, and organized my neighbors around issues like clean streets, and setting up tenant associations in various buildings on the block.

"We also focused on keeping our youngsters occupied. We sponsored job programs each summer and recruited youth workers to do neighborhood assignments.

"Those were difficult but rewarding years. Through our work with young boys and girls we were able to involve youngsters in apprenticeship programs with local businesses, action workshops and tutorial programs.

"In 1968, the year of my divorce from Theroin, I finally landed a job with the New York City Board of Education as an educational assistant. My work schedule at Public School 194 allowed me to have hours similar to the children's school hours. I know it was especially important for me, as a single parent living in an environment filled with temptations, to be there for them.

"During these years, I also was active with a group of parents in the Drew Foundation Headstart program. My children, Gladys and Peter, were attending the program. We all soon concluded that the program didn't seem to be benefiting our children as much as we had hoped, and we decided that we would draw up a proposal to operate our own Headstart Program.

"When we started to think about a name for the program, I suggested the name of the poet Langston Hughes, one of the shining artists of the Harlem Renaissance period.

"Langston had written about Harlem in such a wonderful way. He had been committed. When the Langston Hughes Child Development Center became a reality, Langston had recently died. By the time we were ready to open up, I had a plaque made . . . 'We the people of the community dedicate this Head Start center in memory of Langston Hughes, who contributed spiritually and culturally to the children and people of Harlem.' Poet 1902–1967.

"In time, the Langston Hughes Child Development Center became a model program in the community. Many individuals from the community worked there and many children attended the center which offered a pre-school program on black culture.

"Though I was employed at my job all day, I still wanted to do more for my children and community. I went on to become the parent association president at Countee Cullen School, or P.S. 194 as it was also called, which was located on West 144th Street. While serving as president, I was able to introduce a new educational program called the Gordon Plan into the school. This plan, which featured smaller classes, reading and math laboratories, and parent involvement, was formulated by Dr. Edmund Gordon, a professor at the City College of New York.

"As a result of the program, we were able to hire additional teachers, about seventy paraprofessionals to serve as aides and educational assistants. All of the paraprofessionals came from the immediate area. Later, many of the community workers became a part of the Career Ladder program and went on to become teachers. I served two years as P.A. president and then decided to focus on community development. In this effort, I began working more closely with the block association, trying to improve the social conditions.

"I realized that we had to first improve the housing conditions. I focused my efforts on helping buildings organize to maintain themselves. Drawing on the local churches, I was able to use their facilities for meetings. Some of the ministers and priests began assisting us. From this nucleus, we formed a group called the Community Planning Service, and began raising funds to help buy buildings we hoped to later co-op. Though we were able to grow in the block associations and tenant associations of the neighboring blocks, later we had difficulty making decisions around goals and directions.

"Through my meetings as president of the Parents Association at Countee Cullen School, I met a tall, charismatic man who was organizing Harlem parents to set up an independent school system, and, eventually, the first Harlem High School. His name was Jerome Smith, and he worked with the Congress of Racial Equality. Like my father, he had strong convictions and was a black nationalist.

"At a Thanksgiving party at Langston Hughes, we danced and talked, and Jerome asked me out. During those next months, he became my advocate and lover. Soon he wanted to live with me, but I learned he didn't believe in bourgeois institutions like marriage. He believed in what he called a 'black power' man-woman relationship, a kind of agreement.

"I explained to him I did not want ours to be the beginning of a series of live-in arrangements because I did not want to discredit myself in front of my children. He eventually, but inwardly resentfully, said, 'I do.' We were married in 1968, and had twins in 1972.

"As time went on, I began to feel oppressed. Jerome felt he should take over my social causes, and I should remain at home, a 'submissive wife.' For a while I submitted, but both my resentment and his grew.

"At about the same time, a number of strangers moved into our block. Although I would take my children to the park, I noticed that many of the new mothers would never take their children. They delegated their small children to the streets, and the older ones took care of the younger ones. Or the children would take care of themselves. Sometimes the parents would look out the window to see if their child was all right, but they were never involved in taking them to any kind of recreational activities. As a result, the kids would get into all kinds of trouble.

"I determined, despite all my problems, not to be like them. Everyday, before or after work and on the weekends, I took my kids to one of the parks in the area. I'd pack a snack, take a sand pail, put them in the swings and get involved in their playing. A friend of mine had similar ideas, and on Sunday we'd take our children to the Metropolitan Museum of Art, or the American Museum of Natural History.

"Of course, a lot of my neighbors said, 'My goodness, you're always going out of the neighborhood. Why don't you just send those kids out?' But that wasn't my way. If they were out front playing, I was out there playing with them, and when I wasn't, they had to come upstairs at a certain time, unlike some neighborhood kids who just hung outside in the street until eight or nine o'clock, or even all night long.

"I made sure my children were home, that they had dinner, and I helped them with their homework. Afterward, maybe, they could look at television, or I might even tell them a story.

"You see, that's how I learned—from my parents discussions with me and their telling me stories. And, based on the stories my parents told me, I learned about life and envisioned the wondrous things that I could be. I wanted to inspire my children in the same way. And so, I told my children African tales, such as the one about the little elephant who was much smaller than all the other elephants. Yet what happened? He ended up being one of the bravest and most respected elephants of all.

"I took my role of mother to the children very seriously. But, while my daughter Judy was in high school, my confidence in my role was severely shaken. One day I went into Judy's room. Idly I straightened her bed, picking up the pillow, when suddenly some cellophane packets fell to the floor. Immediately the word 'marijuana' flashed through my mind.

"Confronting her, I learned that Judy was involved with a young man who was selling drugs. Until I found the drugs in my house, I hadn't known what had been going on. Then I knew I had a serious situation on my hands because, being the first child, she set the major example. I was also dealing with her adolescence, a time when a youngster's immediate family becomes secondary. And I understood that peer group pressure is ha-a-a-rd to compete with everywhere, but especially when you live in Harlem.

"Apparently this boyfriend told her, 'Oh, your mother thinks she's better than everybody else and wants to reform everybody.' Hearing this, I realized I had a lot of competition, and I had to be calm and figure out how I was going to play the game.

"That day I just said, 'I love you. I want the best for you.' But a few days later, when we both were less emo-

84

tional, I confided, 'This is very painful for me, but I think you're going to have to get out of this environment. I don't think that you're able to deal with it. And I can't.'

"Part of my mother's family still lived in St. Kitts, my mother's sister, my aunt. She was named Blondina, although everyone called her "Blondie." She was sixty some-odd years old, with a heart condition, and two daughters. We had never met, yet I called and asked her if Judy could come there and stay because the situation in Harlem was so drug infiltrated I feared for Judy's future. And Aunt Blondie said yes.

"Initially, Judy agreed to go, but when I began to make concrete plans for the trip, she reneged. I insisted and used my small line of credit to get together eight hundred dollars to send her off. The morning she said yes, we hurried to get her on the plane. My heart was pounding. I was afraid that when I stepped out of my apartment door I would see that boyfriend of hers just waiting to convince her not to leave this city.

"But as we left our building, I looked up and down the street, and I didn't see him. We jumped into a taxi, and we sped out to Kennedy Airport. While we were there, I felt so angry inside that I was having to send my child away. I thought, Why am I in this situation? Why did my children have to be born in such a terrible environment? It's so unfair.

"When Judy finally took that flight, I felt that a weight had been lifted from me. I said, 'Now I can deal with getting the rest of my family straightened out.'

"I sent my aunt some money to enroll her in school out there. While my daughter was there, my Aunt Blondie passed away, and Judy said she wanted to come back. But I knew I couldn't let that happen. Harlem was the same, and Judy was the same. The combination wouldn't be any better.

"We argued, she stayed on, but eight months later when Judy became eighteen years old, the age of majority, she returned. But when she returned, she was calmer. Then the young man she'd been dating, who had been selling drugs, tried to get in touch with her again. They had a huge fight, and that ended the relationship.

"During this time I worked for the Board of Education. When I finally began working on the administrative level with state urban programs, I decided I really needed a college degree.

"I decided to go to Fordham University, a Catholic college that's based in the Bronx, but that has a campus in Manhattan near Lincoln Center. Fordham offered a special program in social work for adults. I realized with all my responsibilities as a mother and wage earner that I would be taking on a Herculean task. Still I persevered.

"Starting college was exciting. I believed I was standing on the threshold of a new future. I was on my way to becoming a professional, to self sufficiency and improving my economic lot. My children were most supportive and proud. My neighbors felt that it was not necessary for me to go to college, but quietly observed and gave support as far as helping to supervise my children at night when I had to take classes.

"When Dorothy Day heard that I wanted to go back to continue my education, she contacted Eunice Kennedy Shriver, and, as a result, Mrs. Shriver sent five hundred dollars toward my tuition to Dorothy for me. Finally going to college, after so many years of dreaming about it, was exhilarating. In my excitement, I decided I would personally establish 'kinship' with the black giants of arts and letters whom I so admired. Education had been a dear commodity for them; most of the great artists (except Langston Hughes, oddly enough) had acquired at least one degree. They were of the same mind that DuBois was, that African Americans needed a Talented Tenth, or ten percent of our population, who could elevate the race through the professions, industry, and political know-how. Education, to the Renaissance men and women, was a tool that they had argued would lead our people out of the modern-day bondage that blacks were held in even during the heyday of the Harlem Renaissance, the same bondage that we found ourselves in.

"But, at the same time my vision of the past was being enlightened, I also began to notice that the rest of my neighborhood had begun to deteriorate. Buildings were slowly being vacated. The environment of the block was becoming more and more unstable. With all of the ominous changes going on, I became very anxious about my future and the future of my children.

"While this was going on, I was still trying to direct my children in the right direction. But Harlem's negative influences were becoming more blatant. It was difficult to instill in my kids the same values that had brought me to adulthood. Heroin addicts constantly peopled the corner on Seventh Avenue at the west end of my block. The daily panorama of nodding humanity was an awful sight for the young to see and identify with.

"I began to feel discouraged again, like so many people

who live in poverty. Then I began to dream that perhaps the ruin could be restored.

"So I started to organize block residents into a program we called Operation Street Corner. Through this program, addicts on our corner got help at Knickerbocker Hospital where addicted individuals were detoxified. We also tried to involve them in community beautification projects, such as planting gardens and painting buildings.

"All this bettered the rapport and communication between the addicts and some of the residents. As a result, life was a little more bearable for us all.

"I realized that the reason the people who lived in my neighborhood didn't have the feeling of responsibility or pride was because sometimes people's negative thoughts become their own worst enemies. Just as I had learned to project nothing but positive thoughts, my neighbors had bought into projecting negative ones. If you believe the worst is inevitable, you can psyche everybody else into believing it. But there's a verse from the Koran that says, 'If just one person has faith, then the ruin can be restored.'

"I said to myself, 'Things don't have to be like this. Everyone cannot afford to pick up and move. Why the hell do I have to leave the place where I grew up? This street— 143rd Street—can be a Park Avenue; we can have tulips right around here. I have to make my world right here. I can change desolation into some kind of beauty.'

"So I'd pick up broken bottles in the street, and I even decided to plant my first roses.

"When I decided to grow those flowers in the little planter outside my building, some of my neighbors came by to tell me, 'Niggers are going to pull them up.' But I turned around and said, 'If they pull them up, I'm going to plant them again.' It was quite interesting; my community had become comfortable with degradation. My neighbors did not want to give up the myth that we couldn't keep things attractive. Much of our problem as well as many others is, I think, that we don't want to shake off those fated failure myths. And so I became the instrument, and my roses the means.

"Many days I found them lying trampled, but I kept planting those roses over and over again. And small incidents made my efforts worthwhile. One lady brought her three year old girl to sit with her when she'd visit me outside. She told me that my little patch of nature had attracted wonderful little insects, and that her daughter had first seen a bumblebee, grasshopper and caterpillar there. It proved to me that God's creatures would even come to 143rd Street.

"The time came when nobody pulled up the flowers anymore. For me it was a sign my neighbors had accepted the fact that life can be better."

5

Dodge City

"Rita," Mrs. Andrews called.

Rita turned her head slightly, trying to seem alert, but calm. Rita nodded yes.

"Well," Mrs. Andrews went on, "maybe this is all part of it, what you're fighting for, I mean. You can't just give up now.

Rita tried to smile, but her eyes filled with tears. She wiped them away and focused on the decaying streets around her.

"With its burned-out buildings and garbage-strewn lots, 143rd Street and the surrounding blocks in Harlem evoked haunting pictures of Nagasaki after the atomic bombing. Here and there, grimy, sometimes ragged, young men and women peopled the streets, hawking secret wares they promised were available, but not on display. In Nagasaki, they tried to sell their bodies for food and medicine. In Harlem, they tried to corrupt each other's bodies. As many as fifty dealers and lookouts hung out in small areas. Sometimes you couldn't see from one end of the block to the other, the length of a football field, because of all the dope traders and their walk-up customers.

"The most brutal acts of retaliation you can imagine occurred on an almost daily basis. At the other end of the block from my apartment, three men grabbed a dabbler in the trade, threw him up against the brick exterior of an abandoned building and, while he shrieked and pleaded for his life, shot him with a shotgun time after time until he slumped to the sidewalk, dead. Another young man from an adjacent apartment house met an even more gruesome end. He was found dead in a backyard with his testicles cut off. It was then that the neighborhood took to calling the place 'Dodge City' after the infamous Wild West community where similar gunfights and unchecked chaos went on all the time.

"Heroin addiction was at its peak. Cocaine hadn't yet become the drug of choice for poor folks, and no one had ever heard of crack, although marijuana, angel dust and hashish were popular. While it was the most potentially deadly of drugs, heroin also gave that longer-lasting high.

"Overseers tried to keep the peace, but it was impossible for them to get the dealers to co-exist. They would fight over cheating each other. They would fight over who trespassed on somebody else's half-block or block-long area.

(The dealers considered it a no-no to try to sneak around during dealers' off hours to take over their customers.) Some dealers would sell 'beat' stuff. In other words, a dealer would try to skim some money from the dope he'd gotten from his distributor by secretly beating down or 'stepping on' the heroin, in essence, by adulterating it again with lactose. Then, when he'd sold his day's inventory, he'd say, 'I sold your twenty-five bags. Here's your money.' But he may have sold twenty-five bags of his own beat stuff in the meantime. These were the things that got people killed.

"Innocent bystanders were sometimes shot by accident. Old people moved too slowly. Children were found frozen to death, left waiting in abandoned buildings by drugged-out parents who didn't realize how cold it was or how long they'd been gone.

"On two blocks of West 143rd Street, between Lenox and Eighth Avenues, there were thirteen homicides in one year. In the one-square-mile area of the 32nd Precinct, there were about one hundred to one hundred twenty murders per year. It was the most violent precinct in the city. Ninety percent of the murders were drug-related, and so were most of the robberies.

"A constant game of hide and seek was played in the apartment buildings. Dealers would run into the hallways. If you were a resident and were coming into the building, they would threaten and intimidate you.

"Mr. Bell, a tall, sixtyish man, was one of my neighbors. He lived in a rented apartment, in the middle of the block. The building was abandoned except for Bell and another aged lady. The building's hallways had no lights. The corridors were so dark that he needed a flashlight to go in and out. The building was city-owned and without light because no one in charge had bothered to pay the bill. Mr. Bell had lights in his apartment because he paid his bill individually.

"He worked in the city's Human Resources Administration. One day drug dealers took over his whole hallway to sell to customers off the sidewalk.

" 'Mrs. Smith, they're very hostile,' Mr. Bell complained. 'When I come out, I have to beg the little S.O.B.s' pardon to even pass by them. They cuss me out and ask me, 'Hey, ol' man, why you keep comin' in and out of here?' I told them, 'Well, I live here.' And they tell me, 'Well, hurry up then, dammit!' Mrs. Smith, I'm scared of them. They have guns. They'll kill you. I hate to even go home."

"Whenever my children and I saw him coming down the street to go home, I'd ask him, 'Mr. Bell, would you like us to walk you home?'

"He'd reply, 'Yeah, yeah.'

"So, David or I would walk with him, and when we delivered him safely, he'd always leave us with a prayer and a 'thank you' to God.

"Most of the neighborhood buildings were filled with menacing strangers darting in and out of hallways. Fear ran rampant. Like Mr. Bell, most people were intimidated.

"Drugs had been sold in the area for years, but those who used to peddle them had been neighborhood people. And they had done it discreetly, half-ashamed, half-respectfully, totally wary of being arrested. This new group of dope dealers scared everyone to death because they weren't people you knew. No one had the ability to even communicate with them. The street pushing started with outside drug dealers appearing, getting away with selling dope to folks they knew, then to those they didn't. Before anyone knew it, they got bolder, and the neighborhood was soon being overrun by drug people of all ethnic backgrounds who had no relationship with the local people. They came in and set up a market, up and down the streets.

"One of the dealers, Leroy 'Nickey' Barnes, had been a poor Harlem boy who had gotten hooked on heroin during his teens. Nicky had kicked his own habit, but then masterminded what the police said was Harlem's first major heroin operation run by blacks.

"In the early 1970s, it was still the Mafia which was actually importing already refined heroin from various countries. From New York, buyers of large quantities would step it down and sell it across the United States. When it went, it was diluted again. Today, we have all sorts of different ethnic groups that handle narcotics, but, twenty years ago, the Mafia and the large-scale organized crime groups were the main game in town. And they were very, very careful about who they distributed their material to because they didn't want to be tracked.

"Nicky Barnes maneuvered himself into a leverage position with the mob so that he could 'do business.' By the mid-1970s, he controlled heroin in Harlem which, at the time, was the largest retail market for heroin in the world.

"Barnes, who was stocky and round-faced, came across as a well-spoken, educated person, although he had the stereotypical hustler's taste for a closet full of fine suits (reportedly three hundred, custom-made), long limousines and night life. While he eventually graduated from doing dirty work, he had been arrested for murder and possession of a gun, as well as bribery, and a slew of drug charges.

"Like all successful drug lords, Barnes' genius was his ability to distance himself from his street level operation and, thus, keep the police from putting together any real evidence against him. At the same time, since he was so high-profile, he gained a mythical reputation in Harlem as 'Mr. Untouchable,' a super-hip criminal who was so smart and rich that he could shake any court indictment. He was a god to young kids gone bad; he was a nightmare for their mothers. 'So crime doesn't pay, huh? Look at Nicky,' the kids would say. Nicky Barnes had impacted on so many lives that he was once profiled in the *New York Times Sunday Magazine.*

"His mistake may have been bragging that he would never be convicted. He antagonized police and federal agents alike. In 1978 they nailed him, on the unusual federal charges of narcotics racketeering and conspiring to sell millions of dollars of heroin. That "Mr. Untouchable" had been caught and convicted struck everyone as unbelievable, but narcotics agents had finally pieced together evidence from informers in his network who had given him over in exchange for immunity from prosecution.

"To those convinced he'd find yet another angle, his sentence—life in prison with no chance for parole—was unthinkable. The sentence stuck even though Nicky, in an attempt to win a reduced sentence, later fingered more than forty-eight people on the outside, a fourth of whom were convicted. With Barnes behind bars, however, the subsequent vacuum in power opened a flood of opportunities for anybody shrewd enough and violent enough to take his place.

"When Nicky was sent away to prison in 1978, a bloody war broke out over territorial rights. One of the mid-level groups which moved in was the Black Sunday Gang. The Gang consisted of between five and ten heroin traffickers. The thirteen million dollars per year operation that Black Sunday ran on West 143rd alone made it one of the largest heroin distributing blocks in history.

"Black Sunday was actually one of several groups which controlled little fiefdoms throughout Harlem. In West Harlem, there was the Ray family, the relatives of Gene Anthony Ray, the actor-dancer who played 'Leroy' in both the 1980 movie and the subsequent TV series *Fame*. Anthony wasn't involved, but his mom, Jean Ray, his step-father and his grandmother were arrested for large scale heroin trafficking. According to reports, they not only sold to street dealers, they had trafficked in 'weight' to major distributors who moved across the country.

"The Rays were said to operate a multi-million dollar operation that controlled 8th Avenue in lower Harlem all the way up to 155th Street. *The New York Times* called the heart of this stretch the 'drug capital of the east coast.' The area got a lot of publicity in 1979 when David Kennedy, son of Senator Bobby Kennedy, was robbed of thirty dollars at a known heroin buying location, the Shelton Plaza Hotel. A few years later young Kennedy was photographed in Harlem coming out of another heroin spot, and the picture was run on the cover of *People* magazine. Not long afterwards, he had to be hospitalized in Boston for complications from his narcotics abuse. Later he died of an overdose. Every day one or two dozen anonymous, impoverished junkies die in this neighborhood, just like David Kennedy, except no one ever hears about them.

"New York Police Department Lieutenant Pete Pranzo, who arrested Mrs. Ray several times for narcotics at one of her bars, said that police had to be very careful dealing with a celebrity's family. At the time, the series *Fame* was at the peak of its popularity, but Pranzo said the media wasn't told much about Ray's criminal family element. Not only did police not want to hurt Anthony's career by revealing that his family was dealing heroin on a big-time scale, but the cops were concerned about repercussions. These were heavyweight people, one popular with the public and clean, the others crooked but powerful, a family on both sides of the law whose money could secure good lawyers.

"Jean Ray and her mother eventually slipped up selling several 'keys' or kilograms of heroin to New York City undercover police. They were arrested and given prison sentences.

"But the Rays were just one spoke in the wheel. In central Harlem, Ronald Joiner and his brother and relatives controlled 7th Avenue for many years. Controlling the section of Harlem from 110th to 150th Streets were Victor Barry and James King, two major street traffickers.

"They called themselves Black Sunday Boys because the heroin they sold was brand-named Black Sunday. Distributors had their own special brand name. That was the way the buyers were assured of the quality of the drugs. Black Sunday was reputed to be the good stuff. Most of the Harlem mixtures of heroin were very strong, the strongest you could get in the country. If you wanted a strong hit— the purest load to be found on the street—you went to Harlem.

"And that's why all the outsiders, the Jersey kids, the Long Island kids, were killing themselves. They would make their buys in Harlem, sneak onto the rooftops, shoot up their dope, and die from overdoses because they weren't used to such heavy loads. The neighborhoods were overwhelmed with the bodies of people who OD'd. In any given year, there could be as many as fifty to one hundred over-doses in the area between 136th to 150th Streets alone.

"Nevertheless, junkies came from all over the city, as well as New Jersey and Connecticut, to buy dope. Sales competition was fierce. Besides 'Black Sunday,' there was 'Red Star,' 'Black Snow,' '3D,' different names for different brands so the customers could know who was selling what where, and which area had the best product. Every distributor had their own stamp code from a stamp pad which they'd get from the stationary store. A little, semi-official-looking imprint that read '3D' or 'Red Star' or whatever the brand was called was stamped on top of each glassine of heroine.

"Touters openly advertised, stopping cars, calling 'Black Sunday!' or 'You looking for Sudden Death?' You could hear them all the way up on the fourth story where I lived. Some touters waited for customers on the corner, others loitered along sidewalks and openly approached pedestrians, or sat on this stoop or in that doorway.

"Michael and Victor had a bunch of other men working for them. Victor Barry was a drug addict himself. He was dark-skinned, basically nice looking, in his late twenties, sort of heavy set, with a short haircut. He wore casual clothes.

"He dabbled in cocaine, but was mainly a heroin mainliner. Different people have different drug tolerance levels. Sometimes Victor would look very, very straight and cleancut. On a weekend evening, he'd be all dressed up and have a limousine driving him around. At other times, in the middle of the week, he'd look completely disheveled. You'd never believe that it was the same person.

"Barry was very soft spoken, but could intimidate

some of the people nonetheless. He'd tell some resident, 'Hey, I heard you called the cops. You're a nice person. You better not be doing that, 'cause you might get hurt.'

"Victor attended school with Judy and knew all my kids. In fact, he had met me when I was working in the school. He would tell my daughter, 'You know, I like your mother so much, but your mother is ha-a-rd on me. Every-time I look around she's calling the cops.' He was sending a message, and I knew it.

"Victor was a slick character; his charming tongue was just a cover. All the dealers were slick. In their trade that was the difference; an ability to talk their way out of jams, to sort out the situations, to know just how to use infor-mants on the streets.

"Hearing of his attempt to reach me through the chil-dren only made me despise Victor more. He and his friends were destroying the neighborhood. And Victor had even been charged with conspiracy to commit murder stemming from a drug deal.

"One day he openly confronted me. 'Now, Miss Rita, you're a nice lady. You gotta give us a break. Oooh, my goodness. The last time you had the police do that sweep . . . Aw, man, Miss Rita, ya gotta lay off, ya gotta lay off.'

"I looked straight in his eyes, 'You better lay off. And you better get off this block, too. Don't say anything to me because you're perpetrating genocide.'

" 'Miss Rita, I'm only trying to make a dollar.'

" 'Yeah? Well, while you're making a dollar, you're de-stroying lives and setting a very negative example for all the kids who live in this neighborhood. Furthermore, you're using kids to hold drugs, to transport them and to look out for the police. You have a lot to pay for, Victor, so don't

100

sweet talk me. There's nothing nice about you. There's nothing kind about you. You're trying to make your money, but you're making it impossible for decent people to live here. You have no business coming here with your drugs. This is where we live, this is where we raise our kids. If you want to deal, why don't you find some red-light district, or go down by the river to do your business? The only reason you're here is because you want us all as your cover when you shoot up and down and whatever.'

"Victor grimaced, 'Aw, Miss Rita, I'm only trying to make a dollar. I can't get a job. They don't have jobs for blacks.'

" 'You can make a job for yourself if you want to,' I countered. 'Other guys downtown sell socks and whatever. Be like them, but don't come here and intimidate people and make our lives miserable.'

"He and I debated back and forth until he didn't have anything more to say, until he was worn down. 'Well now, Miss Rita, you're probably right,' he said, shaking his head. 'Do you know where I can find a job?'

" 'I know several places. Are you prepared for a job? Did you finish high school?'

" 'No. No.'

" 'Do you have any skills?'

" 'No.'

" 'Why don't you start there again? I could make some referrals. You could get your G.E.D. or get into a training program. There are a lot of things you can do besides dealing drugs, Victor.'

"Victor stared at me unconvinced. 'See, Miss Rita, what you don't understand is that I'm selling dope to people who are on dope already. I'm not making them dope addicts. They have the habit already.'

" 'But that still doesn't make it right, Victor. You're using little kids, and you're showing them that this is the example to follow. If you get the chance, you'd make them into addicts so they would be dependant on you.'

"He put up his hand in protest. 'Oh, no. I only deal with old addicts. Somebody has to sell it to them, so why not me?'

" 'It's still genocide. Do you see what's happening to the people here? After the struggle that we had in the sixties, for civil rights and trying to better our communities, you're out here destroying the race and destroying the people other ways. I've seen you doing business in the park. That's a disgrace. That park is named after Colonel Charles Young.'

" 'Who's he?'

" 'He was a colonel in the United States Army, one of the first black colonels. You're disgracing his name by dealing there.'

" 'Well, I didn't know anything about that.'

" 'You disgrace everything around here. Your mother lives right around the corner. Don't you even respect your mama? The old people can't even go in and out of their building in peace. You don't have the right to harass them like you do. If I have my way, I'm going to put you in jail if you keep on. I'm not afraid of you, because you simply don't have the right to do what you're doing. God will take care of me.'

" 'Aw, Miss Rita. Please, c'mon, give me a break. I have to earn a living.'

" 'Well, everybody else in this block is trying to make a living, too. But you're interfering with that by selling junk, bringing all these people here. People are being robbed, buildings are being set afire.'

" 'But, Miss Rita, I don't have another spot to go to.'

" 'That's your problem. But you're going to get out of here,' I said decisively. 'We pay taxes for our streets and services, and we pay rents, and you just come in here and run your little enterprise for free. You think you have no obligation to society!'

"The debate went on and on. It went nowhere. Victor wasn't the only guy to meet up with 'Miss Rita.' There was James King, whose nickname was 'Fat Mike.' Mike was Victor's 'bull' so to speak, a bodyguard who would do Victor's dirty work. He was known to carry a gun on occasions. He was a heavyweight, stocky fellow about the same age as Victor. Mike wasn't as sharp as Victor Barry, so Mike stayed in the background a little more.

"Victor Barry and James King had been arrested at least thirty times for narcotics sales and possession, and gun charges. Because of their heroin profits, they could afford to live in several different places. They had a place a few blocks from 143rd Street, and they also had apartments in the Bronx where they would distribute heavyweight material. They had safehouses throughout upstate New York. In New Jersey, they had contacts who would put them up when things got too hot in the city. It was only people like the families on my street who were trying to live decently and raise children that had nowhere else to go.

"At the beginning of 1979, things really started to go downhill. An article in the *Village Voice* newspaper said 143rd Street had become a 'major drug outlet.' While covering the story, the *Voice* reporter observed an incident that was commonplace. About fifty 'scramblers' or lookouts loitered on the sidewalk and in front of all of the residents' buildings. These people would yell 'Yo!' loudly when police came into the neighborhood. Some lookouts, blocks away, would use walkie-talkies and radio people who were actually at the drug location so they could close up shop the minute the police were seen.

"In a large scale, quick operation, the moneymen would point to a fellow who actually collected the money. From there the buyer would be directed to the place to pick up his narcotics. It was all done very quickly, very smoothly. The buyers would be lined up. Within five minutes to an hour, dealers could sell fifty to a hundred thousand dollars worth of dime and quarter bags of heroin or cocaine. In an hour, hundreds and hundreds of bags would exchange hands. None of the sellers prolonged their operation for too long a period because it would give more opportunity to get caught. And they also picked their times carefully.

"The heroin addicts in the area knew about the sales on a daily basis. Buyers from out of town or from out of state would come along, stop and ask people. The lookouts and steerers would point them to the right addresses.

"The person who held the money was one step above the person who held the narcotics. The people who handled the street narcotics were the youngest—dealers tried to keep street handlers under sixteen years of age. If they were caught, it was a juvenile offense, no big deal; they were not going to do heavy time. So it was the eleven, twelve and thirteen year olds who actually handed out the glassines of heroin or foils of cocaine.

"The money person would be a little older with a bodyguard armed with knives and guns standing nearby. Then there was an overseer. An overseer was somebody located on the set or just off the street. He would sit in a car at one location or be nearby where he could watch the operation. Other people would report back to him. The overseer never handled the substance other than bringing in a quantity in the middle of the night and getting it sorted and handed out to the middle distributors for the next day's work.

"Besides lookouts, there were steerers or touters like Cleo, the woman on the street the day my son David had been shot. They actually took the customers by the hand and brought them over to the moneyman. On a glassine of heroin, the profit was ten dollars. Of course, it had been stepped down to make hundreds of percent profit. But the person who handled the narcotics got a dollar for every bag that he sold. They in turn would give some money to the steerers. The young children would get fifteen or twenty dollars a day for acting as lookouts.

"The recklessness of the pushers was incredible. One afternoon, a well-known dope dealer found another young man sitting on the hood of his Cadillac. I guess he took offense as a sign of disrespect, or maybe he had previously had a beef with the guy for some other reason. All I know is that there in broad daylight he pulled out his revolver, and in full view of us all, he SHOT! SHOT! SHOT! the legs of the offender. Blood flowed everywhere. The neighborhood was in shock.

"One man in my building was so afraid of the gunslinging that he had to take a drink before he could go onto the street. When I came home from work I had to stop and look around the corner to see if anybody was shooting. Only if I was sure that everything was cool, could I come into my building.

"When you can't go out into the street without peeping from left to right out your door, your freedom has actually been denied you. Plus I knew that these individuals would actually maim me if I got in their way. We were under an attack as real as in any war zone. You can't stay in a state of crisis like that. "I have to move from here," I thought to myself. But I didn't have the money.

"I heard gunshots every night. On several mornings, my neighbors or I found dead bodies in the backyards, a few of them bodies of murdered youngsters who had grown up with my children.

"Then too, the threat of a fire racing down the block and trapping us in our building was also becoming more imminent because the junkies stoked open fires to keep warm. Every night it seemed there was a fire in one of the abandoned buildings. To shoot their heroin, a lot of the addicts went into the vacant shells, where they cooked their fixes, which is to say they lit matches, boiled the heroin and water on spoons, and sterilized the needles using match flame. Sometimes the drug users would go into their nodding trance or pass out before extinguishing the matches, which also accidentally set off fires.

"I can't tell you how many times I saw the light from those golden-orange flames up the street dance on my bedroom walls. Each time, I'd panic momentarily. Then I'd rip off the covers and bound to the floor.

"By this time, we'd gotten accustomed to worrying about fire possibly spreading to our apartment. So right by my bed I kept my little bag of irreplaceable belongings, with a few important papers. Time and again, I've pushed my children down the hallway stairs as we ran out of our building.

"Once downstairs and on the sidewalk, I'd stand and wait with only my nightgown on, and my bag under my arm as firemen put out a trash fire in the building next door.

"Many days I would come out while praying, "The Lord is my Light and my Salvation. Whom shall I fear?" Then with my spiritual boost, do you know what I would say to the first dealer I saw? I'd walk up to him and say, 'I see that you're selling drugs here. Now I want you to leave. If you're here in the next five minutes I'm going to see to it that you're taken away. And I dare you to tell me what you'll do to me. You didn't give me my life, God gave it to me.' About that time, the person would mutter something and walk away, having probably decided that I was a little demented. You know like 'How could she have the heart to come out here and say that?'

"One Monday afternoon I came home on the bus after work. I was tired, my feet were hurting. As usual, I reconnoitered the scene before entering the danger zone of my own block. All clear. The discomfort in my shoes made me trudge the sidewalk, but finally I got to my building. Suddenly, as I neared my steps, I could hear the exasperated whispers of two persons inside the door of my tiny, ground floor vestibule, heatedly rushing to complete a transfer of money for drugs before I arrived.

"The reality of the moment took me hurtling through a range of emotions; surprise, fear, then appraisal of what was happening, and finally anger. Now the street had come inside where I lived. Now the deals were being made in my own building doorway. It was more than indignation over the gradual violation of my living space; this non-descript, misguided pair represented my most wretched problem in life.

"The balled mass of feelings welled up too fast in my brain and in my chest for me to control. Like a blacksmith at the anvil, I took a wide-legged stance and raised the hammer that was only my purse. My first blow was an explosive blast of words, the anger of ten, pent-up years bellowing out of me, "Get out of here! Get out of my building! How dare you sell that crap here! Get out, I said, before I throw you out!"

We all three looked at each other for the eternity of a few frozen, silent seconds. I could feel the heat of my stare searing right into them, burning away their callous indifference. They were so shocked at my potentially dangerous, physical posture that they didn't want to risk passing by me and getting whacked. I had raised the living dead with my loud admonishment, however, so they knew that my first-floor neighbors would soon be cracking their doors, and possibly coming out to assist me.

" 'Go on, get out,' I said! I once again awakened them to my command. That did it. The two eased past where I stood, and managed to grab the door handle without taking their eyes off me. Then they trotted out into the golden light of evening.

"Next morning, I looked out the window and there were some more touters, leaning on the supports to my stoop, motioning the dealers when they had a sale to sell their glassines right in front of my door."

"The dealers' businesses boomed on 143rd Street. They offered such a wide variety of substances that hundreds of word-of-mouth customers flocked to Harlem. Eventually, they recruited neighborhood youngsters as young as eight years old to help them. Riding bicycles became a common way of transporting drugs.

"Ten or eleven year olds graduated to more important jobs. They came to be 'yo-ers' on the street to warn when the police were coming. The kids would yell 'five-oh!' when the police were on the block. Some kids earned bankroll-sized per diems for carrying drugs from one side of the block to the other. Drug dealers told the kids lies about big cards and the glamour of the slammer. They showed kids the booty they had accumulated, while at the same time painting for the youngsters a hopeless picture of America where, they preached, it was impossible to make it legitimately if you were black.

"As with most advertising, the dealers failed to mention the drawbacks for their lifestyles. They didn't tell the children that the rewards of the drug trade were really no rewards at all. That you can pay with your life for fast money or end up spending it for bail, or that a marijuana or heroin high could ultimately dump you back on the same dilapidated doorstep when the ride was over.

"The open market, with its terrible role models for children and its senseless murders, took a tremendous psychological toll on people living on the block. Buildings that were once filled with families started emptying out. Many of the block's apartment houses became completely abandoned. The blitzed-looking hulks became homes to heroin junkies."

6

Human Possibilities Day

Finally Rita reached Harlem Hospital. "Look over there up the street," Mrs. Andrews said, her voice lifting. "There's a parking spot right out front. Now, that's a sign, Rita, if I ever saw one."

"Lets hope so," Rita said and quickly pulled into the space. For a moment she sat completely still, gathering her courage.

"*B*ecoming more involved in social work studies meant reading about people and communities improving their future. So, I wondered . . . why isn't anyone concerned about the housing deterioration in Harlem? Why is nothing happening? All around us they're just building and passing us. This area was never designated as a neighborhood preservation area or anything else. And those are the things that I questioned. And when I did approach the city planners, one said, 'There's nothing that we can do up there. 'Cause in that area there are too many social problems.' He told Mrs. Russell, Mrs. Alvaragna and myself that unless we did something to change the area or get the drugs out, they were not even thinking about building anything there. So we had no choice. Either we had to pick up and go, or they would want to come up here and bulldoze all the problems away.

"So, perhaps I was dealing with a lot of things that I didn't even know about in relation to what was happening in Harlem, and why this area was such a cesspool. Many times I would look at our neighborhood and I'd see so many youngsters on drugs I'd be discouraged.

"Jimmy Carter was president, and everybody in the social work field was focusing on programs for the South Bronx. I said, 'Oh, my goodness. Nobody is thinking about us anymore. Harlem has had its day.'

"No one was really concerned about the programs that were still desperately needed in the Harlem area. That meant it was even more difficult to arouse the interest of the people who were in power. And, of course, there was limited money.

"But I did not give up. I said, 'Well, maybe there's some existing money that can be used.' And, of course, there were a small number of programs that the city operated and some agencies already committed to improving drug-ridden neighborhoods. I began writing to all these people. It

112

seemed endless. I contacted everybody connected with these programs, made appointments with them, went to see them. Then I drew up a plan. In it I wrote about the services we needed on our block.

"Then I thought about the churches and getting them involved and making them a part of it; so I contacted several of the churches in the community and asked for meeting spaces and just sent letters to everyone. You know, when you're out in the world working with organizations that are operated and managed by whites, there are some benefits in that you learn how they operate to resolve a problem.

"In the past, I had the opportunity to work in agencies of that kind. And I used to observe how they operated. They got all of the people that were responsible for a particular type of problem around a table at one time. I took the skills that I had gained and I said, 'This is what I'm going to do. I'm going to get everybody here at one time. Now, who is responsible?' The commissioner of housing, the police department, someone from the mayor's office, someone from the borough president's office, this one, that one, the local politician, the city councilmen, whomever, the district leader and maybe a representative from this particular block, a representative from the particular unit within the department that focuses on narcotics. I wanted to upgrade the quality of life.

"So I got them all lined up. We met at Mother Zion A.M.E., which was the church that I attend. Reverend McMurray was very helpful. I would call him to write letters to Fred Samuels, our former councilman. He would write letters to various departments to assist me in things that I wanted to do. And I had outlined a plan, saying that there were certain things that we had to do. So the city said, 'We're not going to send more money there because the social problems are so terrible'.

And I would get on them and say, 'You like to bulldoze problems away. You knock down everything, and you sweep everybody out, and you call it urban renewal.'

"Trying to get influential people to support and back up the kinds of things that I talked about was unusual in Harlem. Usually in Harlem we don't get our facts together and present a plan to the man. The man always has one for us, which is to knock us down and bulldoze us away, and say that we're responsible for our own problems. They like to blame the victim. But I wouldn't accept that. Not in this case.

"And I planned more meetings. I also felt that I needed to have, as part of the organization of the area, a particular day that we could focus on in reference to our possibilities.

"I decided to call this particular day Human Possibilities because human possibilities are enormous. I said we're going to get a theme, because it was the kind of thing that I noticed from what I had read and I had been taught that African people do when they celebrate. And we were going to celebrate what the future would bring if we all worked together.

"So, my first Human Possibilities Day was April 11, 1979. I wanted all the people from my neighborhood there because we are all taxpayers, and that's what I said to the members of my community. 'I don't care if you get a welfare check or not. Adam Clayton Powell had said when he was alive that it's in your hands.' Then I would quote Malcolm to inspire people. Since I am a good speaker, I tried to put it all together; top it with a little bit of Frederick

Douglass, mix up the pot and talk to them about what's really possible when people work together.

"For our special day we planned a big celebration with a tour of the apartments. People in the neighborhood made all kinds of delicious ethnic dishes. For the small children we planned games and prizes.

"We had a stage, a big stage for speakers, and for dais guests. I sat there along with the others and then afterwards the kids used the stage for performing African dances and Caribbean dances and just plain rocking.

"It was corner-to-corner sound. A loud speaker boomed the music. We had a band, we had a disco. People came from all over the Bronx who knew the area and participated. The street was blocked off. David Dinkins was the city clerk at that time. He came, and so did Fred Samuels, of course, who was the councilman who had worked for us and had worked very hard to put money in the budget so that we could have a better future. Other politicians came as well.

"Andrew Stein showed up. He was very instrumental in later helping us get on HPD to give up the buildings. No mayor had actually come up to a little area like ours, to a grassroots celebration, but I invited him, and Mayor Edward Koch came.

"Now I knew, of course, that Koch was having trouble with black New Yorkers—many of whom felt he was racist —but I realized at that point that no one in the black community was dealing with the issues. They would say that he was this, he was that. But no one presented a plan to say, "You are the mayor. And you're responsible to everyone in the city. I don't care what your feelings are. You have to do

a job. I want to know, what are you going to do about this?"
No one used that approach.

"Several months before I had met the Mayor at his
Constituency Hour along with some of my neighbors, Mrs.
Russell, Mrs. Alvaranga, Anne Ashford, Samuel Wilder and
Marvin Leach. They were all residents of 143rd Street. As
we approached the meeting I saw there was a picket line
outside. But my feeling was, Koch's going to be here for
four years or whatever time and I thought that what we
needed to do was really present our problems to him. He
won't know what I want if I'm outside in a picket line. I
don't think that we all have to use the same means to accomplish the same end. We all may have a major focus, but
we all have to be supportive of one another.

"And I passed a number of people, even my ex-husband standing out there. Nobody wanted to even go up and
talk to the mayor. But I went on in.

"One of the reporters, Gloria Rojas, asked if I didn't
think Koch was prejudiced. I said, 'I really don't think that
he is. I do feel that he is culturally deprived.' I used the
basic kind of common sense that you learn from your el-
ders. Sometimes when you're in war, you have to be diplo-
matic. I figured this was one of the times when presenting
myself with hostility and in a negative manner would not
have helped. One thing that I think is that if we are advocat-
ing for the people, that we have to present ourselves in a
way that we can communicate the needs of the people.

"Now I can get my thing off and call him a sack of
m.f.'s. But the only thing that would mean is that I could
come home and feel satisfied. I wouldn't get anyplace. This
is the way that I have presented myself all along, and I

116

would take others to task. I'd say, 'You have this available . . .'"

"As a result of our initial meeting, Koch apparently said to one of the commissioners, 'Let's see what we can find for this area. Let's do a study.' "

7

Harlem Hospital—A Vigil

Rita, Mrs. Andrews and Mark walked silently toward the hospital entrance. Suddenly the flashing red lights of ambulances and the wailing of police sirens broke the train of Rita's memories. The sound made her wince.

"Are you all right," Mrs. Andrews asked lightly touching Rita's shoulder.

"All right," she repeated mechanically, stoically; but, of course, she wasn't. How could she be?

This was about David, her son. He had been shot, perhaps seriously. He might be dead. She shook the thought off. No, he couldn't be. Mark had said he was running like hell. She smiled despite herself. That sounded like David. He had darn good instincts and some common sense. Those were two things she had seen to it that her kids had. Knew they had to have to survive. Still, children shouldn't have to grow up too fast, as hers had, always wary and stealthy and afraid. Parents shouldn't have to fear for their children's lives everytime they left their apartments.

By the time the three of them reached the emergency room information booth, she was boiling over in anger. "I'm the mother of David Smith," she snapped to the triage nurse on duty.

A monotoned voice answered, "He's back there." The nurse pointed to a wider area connected to a series of small examining rooms at the back of the emergency room, "The last room."

As Rita, Mark and Mrs. Andrews made their way back to the room, a middle-aged man in a dark blue suit approached Rita, partially blocking her passage. "Mrs. Smith, I'm Detective Roberts. I've seen your picture in the newspapers."

She stared uncomprehendingly. "I have to see my son," she said. Her voice rose tearfully, angrily, "He's been shot."

"I know, Mrs. Smith. I'm here to help you. Please calm down. The doctors are working on your son. They don't know where the bullet is, whether it has exited or still is lodged somewhere in his head."

A further cry escaped her throat.

"Why don't we go over there with your family and sit down." He pointed to a small group of chairs in a nearby alcove. "Then I'll go and find out what I can."

"I don't want to sit down," Rita said determinedly. "I want to see my son."

"Please," the detective entreated.

"I know why you're here," Rita spat out. "It's because I've gone public about my dissatisfaction with your precinct and now you're concerned that something the police should have been able to prevent has occurred anyway. Well, you can bet I'm not going to keep quiet about it. Not now. Not ever." She rushed on, her voice breaking, "This is my son, you know."

The detective looked at her miserably. "Mrs. Smith, I know you have the right to be upset, but you have to calm down if you're going to help your son."

His words were true. She knew it. Somewhere within her that strength on which she always could call, which had helped her forge ahead alone, on welfare with her small children depending on her, to get first a college degree, than a graduate degree at Fordham, and later a job as counselor for the Bayville Correctional Facility for Women, surged up. She was beginning to make her presence known in New York City, to deal effectively with the authorities of New York State, as well as with the pimps and drug dealers and prostitutes who'd corrupted her neighborhood. That toughened spirit flowed through her now, quieted and tempered her anger, as well as her fear.

"Of course, you're right," she said with dignity. "We'll sit over there. Find out what you can."

The detective nodded and excused himself. A few minutes later he came back. "Mrs. Smith, be calm, please. They think the bullet may have lodged in the base of David's brain."

Mark gasped.

"Oh, my Lord," Mrs. Andrews cried.

The detective's words struck Rita like a blow.

"My God," she prayed, "I don't deserve this. David doesn't deserve this."

The detective sat down next to her. "They're doing everything they can to find the bullet. He's awake. He's not unconscious." He took a deep breath. "That's a good sign, I think."

Rita said nothing. Did not trust herself to speak. She turned her chair to watch the hands of the clock mounted on the wall. Stared at it while she prayed that David's pain would not be too great, nor hers. Out loud she began the Lord's prayer, "Our Father, who are in heaven . . ." The detective, Mark and Mrs. Andrews joined her. Slowly, the clock's hands moved. It was now eight o'clock, then eight-thirty. She continued to pray. No one came. She looked around, frightened.

Finally, the detective said, "I'll check again. Let me see what's going on."

When he came back, he said excitedly, "The bullet's not in the base of David's brain. When David was spitting out blood, the doctor found tiny fragments of the bullet. It had shattered. He lost some blood, a few teeth, but he's got a strong chin. You made your children real strong."

"Thank God," she sighed, bowing her head. "I know this has to be from Your Power."

A white-coated young doctor with dark hair and a long nose walked toward them. "Are you David Smith's mother?" he inquired politely.

Rita nodded.

"He's going to be all right. He's lost a good deal of blood and a few teeth. The metal splintered in the tongue.

There's some swelling, and we'll need to keep checking his vital signs for two or three days, but he's very lucky; it could have been much worse."

Tears spilled down Rita's face. "When can I see him?"

"I'll take you to him," the doctor said smiling.

"His mother only," he said, gesturing toward Mark and Mrs. Andrews. "He's still pretty weak from the loss of blood and the trauma."

Rita followed the doctor into the small examining room. David lay on the table, an IV attached to his arm.

"Okay, tough jaw," the doctor kidded him, "your mom wants to see the damage."

David smiled groggily, his mouth swollen and bloody, a space where teeth used to be.

"He's not pretty," the doctor teased, "but he's going to be fine."

As soon as she saw for herself that he was going to be all right, a flood of relief washed over her. At the same time, she still worried about David. What was this boy feeling after such a traumatic experience?

David had always been the most ambivalent of her children. Defiant about her activism, he was a complex, sensitive person. Moving first one way and then the other, in between right and wrong, he struggled with growing up poor and black in Harlem, his peer pressures conflicting with his mother's teachings. It was David who had said just a few days ago, "If what you're saying is so right, how come all the bad guys are doing so good?" His words had left her feeling tired, depressed and wondering if it all was ever going to come out as she hoped and prayed.

And now he was here, a victim of having followed her rules, speaking out, protecting his brother.

She watched him closely. He didn't seem angry. Unable to do more than mumble, he looked into her eyes and patted her hand. With the other, she wiped her tears away. He was trying to console her. This boy, her son who had come very close to dying.

And what about his brothers and sisters? Was this an isolated incident or a planned warning to her family? Would her other children be in danger, too? And what about the neighbors she'd stirred up to fight back against these drug pushers? It's one thing to lead a cause you believe in. But first and foremost, she was responsible for her children's lives and safety.

Dark thoughts raced through her mind, but she pushed them away, trying instead to concentrate on her joy that David was going to be well. She would think of the rest later when she was alone.

The doctor turned to her, "Mrs. Smith, we're going to move him to a room now. You can come back tomorrow afternoon. He really needs to sleep."

She nodded. "David, I love you. I'll be back tomorrow." He tried to speak. "Just rest, honey," she said to him reassuringly.

After she rejoined Mark and Mrs. Andrews, they tiredly made their way to the outer waiting room. To her surprise, some of David's friends waited there.

"We were there," Daoud said emphatically.

"Any help you need," Sharif interjected.

"We'll be your witnesses. Just tell us where to sign up," Aziz joined in.

For a time Rita stood very still, not answering, taking it all in, allowing the remarks to wash over her, revitalize her and cleanse the fear, which had spread over her that night.

All she could manage was a murmured thank you as they offered to go back to her apartment and take care of her family.

"I want to go with them," Mark said.

She nodded.

As she drove through the streets, she was still silent. Mrs. Andrews seated beside her followed her lead. After she dropped Mrs. Andrews off, she concentrated on the road. All that had to be said, to be done, was in the past and in the future. Now was a moment to pause, to see and not to see, to hear and not to hear. It was a moment of joy for herself and for David whose life had been spared. Soon enough the rest would catch up with her.

The respite didn't last long. When she pulled into the garage across the street and got out of the car, rapid fire questions began to flash through her mind. What really happened? Why was David shot? Could it have been a mob contract? Was it because of her anti-drug crusade? Were her other children targets? The details of the incident were unclear. Mark obviously didn't know much, and David couldn't speak. How was she going to sort it all out? Decide what to do next? Should she stay in Harlem and fight it out or leave? That was the real question. The one she couldn't avoid or evade.

"Lord, give me light," she mumbled. As she crossed Lenox Avenue, passing under the lamppost, she couldn't help smiling at the coincidence. She paused there for a moment to take a deep breath. Watching her shadowed reflection, she straightened her back trying to maintain a certain presence. She was all too cognizant that her sense of presence was important now, would be reported by those who saw her to those who didn't. With intense effort she kept her head high, stepping forward proudly and surely, just as her parents had taught her. But within, her stomach gurgled, fear and uncertainty bubbled up.

From the corner of her eye, she saw the people at Jerry's Bar craning their necks to view her. She kept on going, vaguely aware that a group were gathered on her apartment house's stoop. As she drew nearer, she recognized Mark and David's three friends who had been at the hospital. From nowhere other young men stepped forward to join them.

"We're going to support you, Miss Rita," one said.

"Just tell us what to do, Miss Rita," another responded.

Amazed, she looked around realizing that this was the group she had tried for so long to help. The young. Before this night some had been openly antagonistic to her, already snared by the drug dealers' lores, and yet here they were when she needed them most. Tears sprang into her eyes.

This was her home. Where she was born and raised. This block. And when she had moved back here she had some mixed feelings, but she had made progress, moving her plans for rebuilding the block forward. Even had some impact on the drug dealers. The neighbors had taken to calling her Miss Rita. A kind of endearing southern treatment of her name. In the black community, putting a "handle" on someone's first name is a sign of warm respect for that person, usually reserved for grandparents and elderly loved ones. During this time her neighbors had seen her struggling, raising seven children, even when accepting welfare still holding her head high. She spoke out loud and often. Some said too often. But even from those she had earned a kind of grudging respect.

By the time she reached the door to her apartment, she felt weary, but better. The shooting couldn't have been a "hit" because some of the guys who were on the doorstoop had been the very guys selling drugs in the area. By expressing their sympathy, they had also silently conveyed to her the fact that David's shooting had been an isolated incident.

Quickly she stashed her briefcase on the living room couch and sat down for a moment at the dining room table to gather her thoughts. The children, hearing the noise, rushed in from their room, surrounding her, kissing her, then taking the other chairs. They all joined her around the table.

"Mom, is David okay?" Gladys asked frowning.

"Is he bleeding, Mama?" Ayana said worriedly.

All kinds of emotions rushed to the surface from within Rita: anguish, pain, remorse, insecurity. These were her children, those she wanted to protect. Those this incident had most wounded. She began to voice her own concerns, trying to get a sense of what they were really feeling. And for the third time that evening she heard voices of support.

"We're not leaving," said outspoken Abena, one of her seven-year-old twins.

"Don't even think of it, Mama," Ayana chimed in.

The usually happy-go-lucky Gladys called out, "No way!" bringing in a pitcher of apple cider and pouring it into heavy cut glasses before handing them out. For a while they sat together quietly, each lost in thought.

It was Rita who broke the heavy silence. "We'd better go to bed. Tomorrow I'll visit David. He'll have had time to think about all this, and we'll see how he feels."

8

Day Light

---

*A*ll morning long Rita concentrated on busy work, the groceries, the errands, the children's homework, willing the afternoon to come so she could see David. His words would be of paramount importance as to whether she would leave or stay in Harlem.

Leaving her apartment house to get her car, she saw strange new faces leering at her on the corner of Lenox Avenue, catty cornered from her building. Judging from their tough dress and stance, she knew they were part of the drug scene. Mrs. Alvaranga, one of her good friends, waved from the door stoop of her own building. Waving a greeting in return, Rita walked over to speak to her.

"You know," Mrs. Alvaranga said, "I don't know what they're selling, but I've seen them make a lot of transactions on the corner today."

As they got nearer Rita saw a woman with the swagger of a man and the leather jacket to match, glaring at them. Defiantly the woman walked across the street where they were standing.

"Hi," she broadcast in a snarl, loud enough for her cohorts to hear. "How are you? You look very nice today."

Rita looked at her apprehensively, silently. It was Cleo. The woman who had caused Rita's son, David to be shot. "What do you want?" Rita asked coldly.

Cleo leaned forward, half-whispering now. "Anymore trouble from you and, if you go to the police, we'll get your younger son, too."

Rita stared her down and Cleo turned on her heel and strode away.

Rita began to feel very leery. She was sure another battle was coming. It was obvious that the new drug dealers had decided to deal with her personally. By setting up shop right across her street—in effect, right in her face—they were challenging her directly.

"Do you know who she is?" Mrs. Alvaranga asked.

Rita nodded. "I know," she said. "And by coming over here to speak to me she's putting me on notice. I'd better watch my back," she whispered saying her good-bye to Mrs. Alvaranga and walking to the garage. There was little time to think of the full meaning of her exchange with Cleo. It was time to begin the short nerve-wracking drive to the hospital.

Rita heard the laughter as she came down the hospital corridor. Much to her surprise, David was sitting up joking with his three roommates. As she walked into his room, he called out, "Mom, come give me a kiss."

He grinned. She winced. His face was swollen. Black and blue and yellow marks covered his jaw, and she immediately saw the space where several teeth used to be. She bent over to kiss him on top of his head.

"You're quite a sight," she said, tears springing to her eyes.

"Mom, it's okay," he replied, looking into her eyes. "I'm okay. God has favored me or else I wouldn't be here."

She nodded, afraid to speak, relishing the moment. David's faith had always been shaky, unlike her own. She wondered if this had been God's way of strengthening it.

She sat down on a scarred, wood-folding chair which had been placed bedside. "Tell me all about what happened yesterday," she said softly, watching him intently. "Tell me what you were thinking."

"What was I thinking about?" He ran his fingers through his Afro. "I just seen the light and didn't want to die.

"I never seen the guy who shot me before, but I knew the woman with him.

"She was an old, grimy, dope fiend lesbian named Cleo. Dressed like a man. I knew her name by the drug dealers and people she worked with calling her.

Rita nodded but said nothing about her encounter with Cleo only an hour before.

David went on, "She had a fiery mouth, I don't know how violent she is.

"I was so bent on watching her, I didn't pay the guy no mind.

"But when he pulled the gun and yelled, I knew he was going to shoot me. I'd said to myself, 'Oh, shit, this guy is going to kill me or when the bullet hits me, I could have a heart attack.' It's strange what you think in your mind.

"I wasn't in pain. Maybe I was in shock. My only thought was getting to the hospital to see if he blew my jaw off. I was in good shape from jogging everyday. I wasn't even tired when I got here. I was rejuvenated. I must have gotten here in two minutes.

"I ran into the emergency room where they roll the stretchers in. I went right past the desk, man, I didn't have time to be stopping at no admission desk dealing with ignorant people there. I just had to get to the doctors. I knew where they were. There were a lot of other people there, but my problem was more serious than anybody else's problem at the time. I was shot. I could have died.

"I found the doctors right away. They laid me on a table, and I asked one of them, 'Doctor, how do I look?' He was a black American, brown-skinned, had curly hair, a full beard and glasses. There was another doctor who was light-skinned and tall.

"They asked me where the bullet was. I said I don't know. It had knocked out my teeth. I said I think I spit the bullets out when I stopped to spit the blood out while I was running. I guess a lot of blood and some teeth came out.

"I just felt my chin when I was running. It felt like I didn't have no chin. Like it was numb. Blood was all over my hand. I said to myself, 'Man, you're an ugly guy now because he blew your whole jaw off.' It felt like the type of numbness you get when you go to the dentist.

"The bullet came right out underneath my bottom lip, about an inch away from my mouth. He had a good chance to miss me, I guess I just didn't turn away fast enough.

"The doctors asked me where the bullet went in, and I said it hit me right here. They they gave me a needle and cut my clothes off. I stayed in emergency for what seemed like hours. Then you came."

Rita let him pour the whole story out, not interrupting, not wanting to inhibit his expression of feelings. But when she saw he was finished, she leaned forward and patted his hand. "David, what do you think," she asked tentatively, "should we leave Harlem?"

"Leave?" he repeated, looking at her angrily. "Run away?"

She nodded.

"Mom, that's not like you. And I'll be damned if some grimy dope peddler's gonna push us out!"

"You mean a lot to me," she interrupted. "You and your brothers and sisters mean everything."

"Mom," he shook his head, "we're just going to continue to fight regardless. This ain't gonna stop nothing."

It was encouraging. Because if she had stopped the fight, she knew the drug dealing on 143rd would have only gotten worse. That would have been a sign to the dealers and pushers that they had won the victory. Then sooner or later, someone else would have gotten hurt, or died. Their family had to either pack their bags and leave the block, or they had to stick with the battle.

Rita looked at her son, wounded and determined, lying

in the hospital bed. "You're right, David," she said quickly, decisively, "we're going to fight."

The terrifying thing three days later when David got out of the hospital was that Sonny was still loose on the streets.

Rita watched anxiously as David, her ex-husband Jerome and some of David's friends spent their time conferring on how to get the gunman. At first she was afraid more violence might occur. After all, her former husband was a Garveyite and a black nationalist. David was always saying Jerome was street bad and would throw down. But after a few days it seemed like all talk and, realizing that David had to have some way to vent his anger and frustration, she didn't interfere.

After nearly a week went by without incident and Rita was beginning to relax, she returned home from work to find David and her husband gone. All the twins seemed to know was, "They went to find Sonny." Rita's fears surged.

They finally returned several hours later and Rita pounced on them. "What's going on here? Are you crazy? You'd better tell me everything!"

Jerome's mouth tightened. He said nothing. David's eyes blazed.

"About twenty of us went around to their stores," David said defiantly.

"Who was with you?" Rita asked.

"My stepfather," he motioned toward Jerome, "some of his old buddies from the sixties and all my Muslim brothers. We marched up there and went to see the drug dealers. We went to see the people who were giving Sonny drugs. We went around and told them there'd better not be any more conflict. We went around there ready to kill them people."

Rita echoed his words, shuddering, "Kill them?"

David nodded and raced on. "We went to where they had a couple of stores around on 144th. Candy store, game room, grocery store, about four stores in all.

"It was a nice day, and they were sitting on their cars out in front of their stores with their little girlfriends working inside or whoever they had working. An old faggot named Billy Sims, who had been in the first nation of Islam, I think he was a Farrakhanite, bald head, knock-kneed, slew-footed. That's how I could tell he had been in the nation with them.

"But that's not strange," David shrugged, "Muslims are human. All Muslim means is 'a person who submits to God'."

"I thought you were just looking for Sonny," Rita injected.

"We were looking for the bosses," David went on. "We were armed with guns and shotguns. We had sawed-off shotguns under our rain-and-shine coats. We seen them on the streets.

"I was for murdering all of them. They were all responsible. Maybe about five top people. But Sonny first.

"We could have murdered that man, but there would have been lots of complications from murdering somebody in the broad daylight instead of taking him off at night."

"Like spending the rest of your natural life in jail," Rita said angrily.

"Yeah, that might be one," David answered with a grin. "Anyway, we let them know that there was an incident over the drugs, and we were looking for the fella. Could they assist us. Jerome was doing the talking. He took one of the dealers aside. I don't know what he said, the dope dealer wasn't talking disrespectfully, but his mannerisms were very arrogant. Somebody had to talk some sense because he wasn't worth killing.

"I can't remember the exact words he used, but Jerry," he said indicating his stepfather, "told him there's been some problems. We were looking for this guy, and we heard that he was working for you. We don't want anybody around here selling drugs, or if anybody comes around here causing anybody to get hurt, there's going to be an act of war, but only the next time it was going to involve everybody.

"The guy listened, but he was arrogant. He acted like he didn't care. But, Mom, we had the sense because we didn't murder him and his friends right there. We knew he was ignorant and was blind."

"Did you find Sonny?" Rita asked hoarsely.

David shook his head. "Nope, but we sent out the word we're looking for him. He'll show up; we'll catch him."

The first part of David's last statement proved right. One evening, not long after, David and Rita were in her blue 1971 Marquis sedan driving to the post office. Sitting on the passenger's side, David suddenly spotted Sonny hanging out on the corner by the Blue Angel Bar on 143rd Street and Seventh Avenue. Sonny also saw David. Although neither had seen the other since the shooting, David and Sonny instantly recognized each other. Sonny obviously was capitalizing on the fear he was sure David still harbored after nearly having his head blown off by making a fanning motion with his hand, as if to tell David, "Come on, punk. If you want me, we can have it out right here and now."

David shouted, "That's the guy who shot me!"

Startled, Rita slammed on the brakes and, with the car stopped in the middle of traffic, wildly looked around and demanded, "Where? Where?"

When the car stopped, David panicked, jumping into the back seat. "Mom, I didn't expect you to make me a sitting duck for my attempted murderer to finish me off."

Meanwhile, Rita eased the car out of the line of traffic and parked it to one side of the street. Turning around to point at him, she watched as Sonny moved back into the crowd of passersby. "He probably doesn't know what we're going to do," she said, never taking her eyes off him.

David mimicked him. "Yeah. 'Them damn Smiths . . . with all that marching and preaching. They're crazy. Ain't no telling what they'll do,' he's probably thinking." David's words sounded tentative, as though he was testing the idea.

Staring intently, they finally saw him dart down an alley and take off running.

Quickly Rita drove off. David's head jerked back and forth to see if he could spot Sonny. Finally, he turned to her. "I think he's gone," he said with relief.

Later on, David told people that Sonny had fled "like a scared chicken." But at that moment, on that day, he had been too nervous to say anything like that until Sonny was long gone.

Although Sonny kept showing up unexpectedly in unexpected places, neither David nor the police seemed able to catch up with him. At least not for long.

9

Nowhere to Run, No Place to Hide

*T*he unexpected sharp nip in the air made Rita shiver. It was October already she realized with a start, wishing she'd taken a coat. Pulling her blue linen jacket tighter around her, Rita stepped from the apartment entrance onto the concrete stairs and began automatically to scan 143rd Street one segment at a time. It had been two months since David had been shot. His assailant, Fred "Sonny" Figures, was still out there roaming these streets, still threatening her children and everyone else's, still dealing more drugs. She bit her lip and kept looking. She was pretty sick of the way these dope dealers terrorized the neighborhood. Especially of the way Figures had kept on taunting her family, teasing the police and the searchers by showing up, showing off and, just as they thought they had him, disappearing. She was damned if she wasn't going to do something about it, she thought walking toward the garage where she kept her car. And not tomorrow, today. She felt her old stubbornness resurfacing again.

This morning she was on her way to police headquarters to the first meeting of the Narcotic's Task Force she had fought to establish. The meeting, she reflected, would provide a perfect opportunity to prod the police on the search for David's attacker. That was the only way to get things done when you lived in a ghetto, she reflected. It was all too easy for law enforcement officials to consign violence, even death, to just another every day occurrence, she thought, getting into her car.

Rita shook her head forcefully as she began to drive. Well, they weren't going to consign David's attempted murder to some dusty file box. This time the police weren't going to blame the victim or exercise indifference. There was going to be justice here for David, for her other children, herself and her neighbors. They needed to see Figures prosecuted in order to gain the courage they needed to tackle the even more onerous task of finding a way to drive all these druggies off their block, out of their neighborhood.

By the time she marched into police headquarters she was ready to do battle.

"I'm Rita Webb Smith," she said pausing at the front desk and squaring her shoulders. "I'm here for a meeting with Sergeant Pranzo."

The sleepy-looking officer nodded. "Just a minute. I'll advise him you're here," he said disinterestedly.

"No need to do that," Rita quickly retorted. "I know my way and I'll advise him." Before he could object she strode past him and toward the sergeant's door.

"Pranzo," she said walking in, "I'm here for our meeting."

The dark, stocky Pranzo, who had worked his way up to sergeant the hard way and had been involved in his share of shootings, looked up from his paperwork and grinned. "So I see, Mrs. Smith. You're about a half an hour early. Let me call in my commanding officer, Joe Vincent, and the others and we can begin."

"Before you do that," Rita said forcefully, "I want you to tell me when you're going to arrest the man who tried to murder my son."

"Believe me we're looking everywhere for him," Pranzo said frustratedly. "Everytime we get close, the bastard slips through our fingers."

"Well, I want you to turn up the pressure," Rita said determinedly. "You've got to arrest him."

"We're doing all we can, believe me," Pranzo said earnestly.

"Do more," Rita said. "Get him."

Pranzo nodded. "You have my word."

"Good," she laughed. "But that's not all I'll have if that arrest doesn't come soon."

"I get the picture," he laughed in return. "Look, we're after the same thing. Why don't you sit down please." He walked around the desk and grabbed a pile of files from the nearest chair so that she had some room. "Have some coffee. The machine's out in the hall. I'll be right back."

Rita nodded. "Thanks. I will," she said relaxing a bit. "This morning has winter in its veins."

Pranzo laughed again. "Well we agree on that, too. It's a good omen." He tapped her shoulder lightly as he left.

When he came back followed by a score of detectives, Rita had cleaned off the rest of the available chairs and arranged them in a semi-circle around the desk. "Thanks," Pranzo said cheerfully. "I guess things get a bit cluttered in here."

"Guys, this is Mrs. Smith. She's the community spark which ignited this committee."

Rita smiled in return.

Pranzo began to introduce first his commander and then the detectives to Rita. "He's Jimmy Davis."

"Good morning to you," the young officer said rising.

Rita nodded, her eyebrows raised. Davis was black. Her opinion of Pranzo shot up as she looked around and saw three other blacks on the team.

"And this," Pranzo went on pointing to another detective, "is Hal Davis." He stopped and took a breath. "Listen, the rest of you introduce yourselves to Mrs. Smith."

"I'm John Bailey," a thirtyish copper-skinned detective said.

"Bobby Smith," grinned a stocky young cop who looked like a muscle-clad fighter.

"Don't let his brawn fool you," Pranzo broke in. "He also has a college degree and he's one of the best cops I've worked with on the force."

Rita quickly exchanged greetings with the assembled group and then Pranzo went on.

"Mrs. Smith," he leaned towards her appraisingly, "we've already formulated our first defense strategy against the low-lifes who are running you and your neighbors off your block."

She nodded. "Go on."

"There will be seven of us plus me on a narcotics task force that you wanted to call The Quality of Life team; officially we'll call ourselves the Street Conditions Unit of the 32nd Precinct. We've looked over the long list," he paused and smiled, "of suggestions you've submitted and," he grew serious again, "we're going to make our first raid on your street."

"Inside the buildings, not just outside," Rita insisted.

He nodded, "Definitely."

"And the abandoned buildings."

"Those too, and the drug dens and shooting galleries where there would be hypodermics where they would shoot up all the junkies and shoot up the heroin."

"We can count on their being regular raids, not just a one shot deal," she asked.

"Very definitely," he agreed. "We're going to focus on West 143rd Street."

Rita smiled not completely believing what she heard, but ready to do what she could to make it happen. "When do you begin?"

Commander Vincent looked straight in her eyes. "You sure you want the details?"

"Damn right I do," she shot back. "I want to be there to see it."

He laughed. "Well, you're totally responsible for all this so I guess you've got that right." He dropped his voice. "Thursday at 8 p.m."

Rita shook her head. "That's only three days off." Her voice rose questioningly.

"We're ready," Pranzo firmly declared. The others con-
curred.

"Then I guess I'm ready too," Rita said.

Thursday night Rita stood at her window. She saw the
assigned cops in unmarked cars trying to get into the center
of the block. Some were in livery cabs, others in small
trucks and unmarked vehicles. Even those who moved into
the area on foot were plain clothes cops. The fact that they
were largely white went unnoticed in an area populated as
soon as darkness fell by the many-hued drug addicts who
came here from all over the city and suburbs as well.
Within thirty minutes the police attack began. They sealed
off the whole block and put about three hundred people, if
not more, against the wall. The addicts and dealers touched
hand-to-hand from Lenox Avenue to Seventh Avenue.

As she watched, the police recovered multiple guns
and a large quantity of narcotics. Some of the people were
let go and scrambled through back alleys. But huge numbers were put into cars, wagons, vans, everything available.
For Rita it was a tremendous sight to see everybody, all the
dealers and users, made to respect the law. Of course, it
took some pushing and shoving, and it took a lot of necessary force. Some blood flowed as the dealers and their cohorts resisted the officers and tried to hold their turf.

The officers gave chase as their captives tried to scram-
ble up into the buildings and escape. More had to be sub-
dued accordingly. But the arrests were made quickly and a
half hour to an hour later, order had been restored on the
block and everybody who couldn't fit into the precinct
transportation was cut loose and left the area. Even so, the

police did wind up with a lot of prisoners, drug dealers and their motley crews. At least well over one hundred people.

The residents, especially the senior citizens, were yelling down cheers. And then Rita left her apartment. She came right outside proudly walking down the street and she strode over to Pranzo who was directing the operation and grabbed him. "I don't believe it. I've been waiting for this for years."

For a moment they just stood there and grinned at each other. And finally they said simultaneously, "Yes, it can be done." Rita added, "And this is the beginning."

A week later the police made another raid. Ten or fifteen cops in wagons and cars began to make the hits. Down one street they chased a small, shadowy man who had been seen dealing back and forth through the back alleys almost losing him several times in the chase. Despite his elusiveness they finally caught him and Detective Miller, winded and hoarse, read him his Miranda rights. The man refused to give his name but checking his identification, Miller found he'd made a more auspicious find than the man's sullen but meek attitude suggested.

Fred 'Sonny' Figures was finally under arrest.

WHY?
THE TRIAL

10

Copping a Plea

---

*T*he Manhattan assistant district attorney who was assigned to prosecute Figures was Bob McGuirl. McGuirl was a clean-cut, young, Catholic kid who at the time had only been out of Georgetown Law School for about three years. He was the kind of attorney who had gone into law to try to make a difference.

As a law student, McGuirl had fought tenant cases for the poor in Washington, D.C., but later a professor suggested to him that he bypass the glamourous career of defense attorney to become a prosecutor. His professor had explained that district attorneys call the shots: they either bring the charges or drop them against defendants and they initiate the court action.

Thinking he could do more good in the job of legal initiator, in 1977 McGuirl interviewed for an assistant district attorney's slot in Manhattan, the premier D.A.'s office in the country. Since he had been raised in Oradel, New Jersey, an affluent bedroom suburb of New York City, the job was prestigious in title only. When he was hired in 1977, Bob McGuirl earned all of $12,500 in salary.

By the time McGuirl met with Figures, the detectives from the precinct had already questioned him. McGuirl quickly formed his opinion. "You have a rap sheet as long as your arm," he told Figures. "Warrants for arrests, felony arrests, misdemeanor arrests, you name it. There's an established pattern of being arrested, convicted, incarcerated, released from jail, and starting the whole cycle again."

Figures sullenly remained silent. Finally McGuirl motioned to the guard to take Figures away and walked outside to talk to Pranzo who was waiting for him.

"It didn't take me long to see that I didn't like this guy," McGuirl said, disgustedly. "Look at what he's doing to other people."

"In his case," Pranzo said, "he's singled himself out, distinguished himself in his field." McGuirl nodded. "Yup, the usual profile of a violent criminal is someone who's much younger, probably about sixteen years old. Here's a guy who's in his late twenties. A guy who's still doing this at this stage of his life is definitely a career criminal. He's not going to be reformed."

"I don't know why he's gone this way, nor will I ever know. But I know this: sooner or later Figures is going to kill somebody. For the sake of those around him, Fred Figures needs to be off the street. I want to get not only the attempted murder conviction, but one for persistent felons."

Pranzo nodded. He smiled at the idealism of the younger man but he had to agree with his conclusion.

McGuirl was required by Criminal Procedure Law 1880 to indict the suspect within three court days. This law states that anyone incarcerated who can't afford to pay bail must be indicted within three court days or he is allowed to go free on his own recognizance. McGuirl said he knew if Figures was ever released, he would never be seen again.

He brought witnesses before the Grand Jury to elicit testimony. He explained the law to the Grand Jury and then it voted on whether Figures should stand trial on attempted murder. McGuirl got the indictment.

On November 10th, the court clerk called the indictment proceeding to order. "Present in the court in the absence of any prospective jurors, the Defendant Fred Figures, his attorney, Edwin Paul Gonzalez and present for the People, Assistant District Attorney, Robert McGuirl."

Figure's stocky, publicly appointed lawyer stepped forward. "Your Honor, at this time the defendant wishes to withdraw his previously entered plea of not guilty and pleads guilty to the first count of the indictment, attempted murder, to cover the entire indictment."

McGuirl could not suppress his smile. "That plea is acceptable to the People."

Judge Klein's well-known deep voice resounded in the small room. "Fred Figures, I am going to ask you certain questions, if there is anything you do not understand, ask your attorney, Edwin Paul Gonzalez, who is seated right next to you, or ask the court; is that clear?"

Figures nodded.

Klein went on. "Fred Figures, the crime to which you wish to plead guilty is a class B, namely an attempt to commit the crime of murder in the second degree, and if you have had a previous felony conviction within the last ten years, and I believe you have had in this state, the court would have to sentence you as a second felony offender and the term would be a minimum of six years and a maximum of twelve years, and I will go into that much further in a moment. Do you understand that so far?'

Figures did not look up.

Klein said, "Now, have you authorized your attorney, Edwin Paul Gonzalez, on your behalf, to withdraw your plea of not guilty previously entered and to now plead you guilty to an attempt to commit the crime of murder in the second degree, a class B felony?"

Figures nodded sullenly.

Klein tried to catch his eye. "Under the first count of the indictment to cover everything in the indictment?"

"Yes," Figures said quietly.

"Mr. Figures, before you offered to take this plea of guilty did you talk over and discuss this matter of your pleading guilty to this class B felony with your attorney, Mr. Gonzalez, who is seated right next to you?" Klein entreated.

"Yes," Figures said mechanically.

Klein continued. "Now, has anyone made any promises to you—that is, your own attorney, the district attorney, myself or anyone else, as to what the sentence of the court will be in order to induce you to plead guilty with this understanding, I had a lengthy discussion with your attorney, Mr. Gonzalez, also with the assistant district attorney, Bob McGuirl, and we arrived at an agreement among ourselves which is as follows: When the court receives your probation report and the court finds, after reading the probation report that I had to sentence you as a second felony offender, the sentence of the court would be a minimum of six years and a maximum of twelve years and that that sentence would run concurrent with a prior sentence you had received under Indictment #3672 1979 which herein you pleaded guilty, I believe, to criminal sale of a controlled substance in the fifth degree, for which you are now serving three to six years. In other words, the sentence that I would impose, this six to twelve years sentence for the crime to which you are now pleading guilty would run concurrent, not consecutive. I repeat, concurrent with the crime for which you are now serving three to six years. Is that clear to you?"

"Yes, sir."

Klein said. "Now, if and when I get the probation report back, the court finds it could not give you a sentence of six to twelve years but would have to give you, let us say, a greater sentence, at that time, the court would permit you to withdraw your present plea of guilty, and allow you to put back, reinstate your not guilty plea, so that you would not be prejudiced in any way. Do you understand that?"

"Yes, sir."

Klein did his duty thoughtfully. "And I want to make it very clear to you that the sentence of six to twelve years, assuming your probation report is okay and that I can give you, specifically agreed with myself, your lawyer and the assistant district attorney; is that clear?"

153

"Yes, sir," Figures answered.

Klein said, as if by rote, "And there is no other agreement or understanding off the record between myself, the assistant district attorney or your lawyer, is that clear?"

"Yes."

Klein's voiced firmed. "Now, Fred Figures, are you pleading guilty voluntarily, of your own free will, without anyone threatening you or forcing you to do this, because you believe it to be the right thing to do?"

"Right," Figures said gesturing to get on with it.

"Do you understand that by pleading guilty you are waiving, giving up your absolute right to a trial by jury or by this court on the question of you guilt or innocence?"

Figures answered, his voice flat, "Yes."

Klein queried, "And do you also understand that you are giving up, you are waiving your right to be confronted by any accusing witnesses?"

"Yes."

Klein pressed, "And you also understand that you are waiving, giving up your right against self-incrimination, your right to keep silent?"

"Yes," Figures monotoned.

"You also understand that this plea of guilty to an attempt to commit the crime of murder in the second degree, a class B felony, has the same legal effect, means the same thing as a conviction after trial?" Klein looked at him searchingly.

"Yes."

Klein was clearly getting nowhere. "Now has everything I have said to you or asked you up to this very moment been clear to you and understood by you?"

"Yes."

Klein went on. "Now did you, on or about August 17, 1979 in the Borough of Manhattan, City of New York, with intent to cause the death of one David Smith, attempt to cause the death of David Smith by shooting him with a loaded pistol?"

Figures looked at an invisible spot in the floor. "Yes."

"Well, I will accept the plea," Klein said taking a deep breath.

By the time the hearing was finally over, the self-confessed Figures had been assigned to Rikers Prison. When Rita spoke to the district attorney he told her the date for sentencing was set for December 12th.

On that day she went to the court along with some of her family and neighbors from the community including David's friends to see what kind of sentencing he would receive. They all waited anxiously.

The small courtroom was crowded with spectators when Figures was brought in handcuffed. As the court clerk read the charges, Figures did not look up. Then he was handed the prosecutor's statement.

"Fred Figures, the district attorney of this county alleges by the statement that you are Fred Figures and that on August 21, 1973 you were convicted in the Supreme Court of the County of New York for the crime of robbery in the third degree, a conviction for which a sentence in excess of one year was authorized by law.

"Now, Mr. Figures, you have the right to admit the statements in this allegation—admit the allegations in this statement or deny it. You can assert that the conviction was obtained against you in an unconstitutional fashion. Will you confer with your attorney and advise the court on how you state to this allegation."

155

Gonzalez whispered to Figures for a moment. Judge Klein looked at them. "Mr. Figures, do you wish to deny any of the allegations set forth in this statement that was handed to you?"

Still Figures did not look up.

Klein went on. "The court finds—

The court clerk interrupted. "Does your honor direct that a finding be entered?"

Klein resumed. "The court finds that this defendant is a predicate felon and a finding could be entered accordingly."

The court clerk announced, "Fred Figures, on this indictment 829/1980, you are now being arraigned for sentence on your plea of guilty to the crime of attempt to commit the crime of murder in the second degree as a second felony offender.

"Now Mr. Figures, before the sentence is imposed, the court will permit the district attorney, your lawyer and you, Mr. Figures, each now to have an opportunity to exercise the right to be heard.

Mr. McGuirl?"

McGuirl, in his most serious manner, spoke. "I would note the victim of this shooting, Mr. Smith, is in the courtroom, as are several members of the community who were involved in some of the efforts in this case."

At his words Fred Figures suddenly looked up as if focusing for the first time on his surrounding and when his eyes fastened on Rita, his passive demeanor changed to furor.

McGuirl continued. "Other than that, your Honor is aware of the circumstances of the shooting in this case.

Your Honor has also read the probation report, and I have nothing further to add beyond that."

His lawyer, reading his notes over, did not notice his client's reaction to McGuirl's words. "Just to refresh the court, that there has been a negotiated plea and the court has make certain assurances herein and ask that the court abide by the assurances also the concurrent aspects of the sentencing."

The court clerk broke in, "Mr. Figures, you have the right to make a statement on your own behalf if you wish to do so. If you wish to do so, do so now, sir."

Figures rose shaking with anger but kept his voice civil. "Your Honor, you know, like I pleaded guilty to this case here, you know, because of what, you know, I feel as though the law, you know, requires me, you know, to plead. But I feel as though, your Honor, that I am guilty with an explanation."

Astonished Rita lashed out, "I thought you could only be guilty with an explanation if you got a parking ticket. I didn't think that if you attempted to murder someone you were allowed to be guilty with an explanation."

Laughter broke out in the courtroom. The judge's gavel restored order and the judge allowed Fred Figures to withdraw his plea and set a date for trial. As she left the courtroom Rita felt infuriated. She wanted this to be over with and for this man to receive his just punishment.

McGuirl tried to keep her calm saying, "Don't worry, we'll just go all the way with this one. We'll call all the witnesses who were there and get the medical records. Don't worry, we'll get a conviction."

Yet the case was by no means airtight Rita knew. Mc-
Guirl confirmed there were at least two legal problems.
First was the all-important matter of identification.

Since Figures had just disappeared into the street and
tenements of Harlem, he had not been captured for months
after the shooting occurred. The defense could make a
strong case that David had simply fingered the wrong man.
Would a jury be convinced that David had really gotten a
good look at his attacker at a time when he may have been
overcome with excitement, fear, and finally, pain from having been shot?

It is "the shaky witness identification" that lawyers
never learn about in law school but which they immediately find they must deal with in courtroom practice.

Second on McGuirl's list of worries was the fact that
testimony about the Smiths' anti-drug efforts on the block
was possibly not going to be allowed to be heard because
there was no direct evidence that Figures was a hired gun
to protect Cleo during her heroin dealing. McGuirl had no
right to fingerprint her and he couldn't track her down by
name.

The prosecutor had met Rita and from talking with her
about her family's kicking drug pushers off the street, he
believed David's account of the scenario in that afternoon
fifteen months before. But would the jury?

Finally, McGuirl wasn't sure that Figures would testify
or how Figures could make his legal strategy the plea that
he had shot David Smith in self-defense and to defend Cleo
from assault.

If so McGuirl knew he'd try to give the impression that
he had helped a woman in distress and it would be a beguil-
ing defense.

Anticipating that defense strategy—as well as possible others—McGuirl diligently began to prepare his case. Rita did what she could to help reassure the witnesses and keep David's spirit up. But she, too, was worried.

This was intensified a week or so before the trial when a bronze-skinned man and a honey-complexioned woman, both in dark glasses, accosted her inside the door of her apartment house as Rita arrived home from work. "We're ready to fight you about pushing this case with Fred Figures," the man said menacingly.

"Well, I am going all the way with it," Rita retorted. "So do what you will."

"We'll see and so will you," the two threatened as they left.

McGuirl told Rita he had decided to charge Figures with being a predicate violent offender. If he could prove that the man who shot David was habitually violent, and a menace, he could get him behind bars for between twenty-five years to life. The predicate violent offender rap also put Figures and his defense attorney in the position of having no room to plea bargain. Because of his criminal record and because of the serious nature of the crime, most judges would have no reason to give Figures any reduction in his sentence.

The way McGuirl saw it, Figures would either have to plead guilty or fight the charge in full.

11

The Trial Begins

*O*n the opening day of Fred Figures' trial for the attempted murder of David Smith, the prosecutor Bob McGuirl, having in the interim become a staunch supporter of the battle Rita was waging not only for justice for her son but for her community, set the tone by placing this particular act of violence in the context from which it had sprung.

In a sober voice McGuirl said, "Now, with any trial, any case, it's always best to go back to the beginning and start from the beginning. And the beginning in this case is one 143rd Street and the beginning is narcotics, specifically heroin. You're going to meet some people who live on 143rd

Street and have been there a long time, and intend to stay there a long time. You're going to meet David Smith, the person you heard mentioned in the indictment as being the victim of the shooting. You'll meet Mark Smith and there will be more of the other witnesses you'll hear from. They're going to tell you about 143rd Street. Things don't begin on August 17, 1979, that you have heard four times now in the indictment. It begins a little bit earlier than that, months earlier than that. It begins with an influx, and a heavy influx, of narcotics' traffic into 143rd Street. Sure, it's always been there, it's always been in the area, one place or another, but never until a few months before August 17, 1979, never before anything like this, never before the volume, never before the numbers of people on that street, never before a lot of money changing hands, and a lot of glassines all going back and forth, never before all of those cars from New Jersey, Connecticut, all over 143rd Street."

He gestured toward the spectators.

"There were people living there long before then and there are people living there now. There are residents, that's a neighborhood to some people, that's home to some people. And you'll hear about the Smiths and they were there then when this started and they're there now. And you'll hear it was a family. The family has a youngest and the oldest and you'll hear about the youngest and you'll hear about the oldest. There comes a time narcotics brings more than just narcotics. I don't think I need to dwell on that. There are a number of things associated with that, and they have an effect on a neighborhood. And that volume of narcotics' traffic has an effect on a neighborhood. And that's what began to happen on 143rd Street, right between Seventh and Lennox. Conditions got worse and worse. And you'll hear the Smiths were there. And you'll hear they were there for the duration, better or worse, they were going to be there. No place to move, no place to go, that's their block."

McGuirl strode back and forth.

"There comes a time for everyone when you're going to decide what you are going to do. Well, you can stay in the building, you can lock up the doors, you can get in there as early as you can when it starts getting dark, and you stay there until its light. And I can go on, you've got the picture, or you can take another tact, and that's what happened on 143rd Street. And that runs something like this:

"This is our block," his voice rose forcefully, "we were here before this ever happened, and we will be here when it's over, and this is where we live, this is our neighborhood, this is our home, and we are not moving. And just as easily as those narcotics' dealers and addicts moved in there, this is where we live, so they can move out too.

"Well, there is a police department and there was some effort to reach out to the police department. There is only so much the police can do. And you'll hear more about Mark Smith and Peter Smith and David Smith, and what they undertook on their own to do on 143rd Street. I won't dwell on it because I think they can tell you a lot better than I can." Then McGuirl began to make comments concerning Mark Smith's confrontation with Cleo.

"And this has been going on for months and frankly he's probably had it. And he starts yelling at her for what she's doing. It escalates. He starts out talking, it escalates, and he reaches a point, he grabs her and he still has a hammer, he didn't put it down when he walked over, and he's

holding it up and he's telling her get off my block, no dealing here. I don't want anybody dealing on this block."

He paused for a sip of water.

"Well, in addition to Mark Smith being there, and Cleo
being there, and David Smith, Peter Smith, Mr. Figures was
there. And Mr. Figures was with another man known as
Smoke. And Mr. Figures and Smoke were pretty close to
where Mark and Cleo were. And Mr. Figures sort of ambled
away from the car he was leaning on and began to go over
to where Mark and Cleo were. And David Smith, who had
been standing there, walked over and intercepted Mr. Figures before he got to where Mark and Cleo were. And there
was a conversation there; basically, 'hey, cool it, man, mind
your own business, it doesn't affect you, stay out of it',
something like that. And there was an argument between
David Smith and the Defendant. David Smith punched the
Defendant. The Defendant went back a little from the blow
and then the Defendant brought out the great equalizer,
and the Defendant pulled the gun right out of his waistband
and right at David Smith. He told David Smith, 'M.F., I'm
going to kill you'. And he pointed that gun at his head and
he pulled the trigger and he shot him, dead on in the head.
David Smith ran. He ran to Harlem Hospital spitting out
teeth, part of his tongue, lead from a bullet."

McGuirl pointed toward the defendant.

"Back on 143rd Street, Mr. Figures calmly surveyed
the situation. And you'll hear more about that. And then he
thought maybe it was time for him to leave too. And he
went the other way and he left the block.

"Well, more goes on, that leads ultimately, you'll hear
from Detective John Miller, from the 32 Precinct, to an ar-

rest on February 19, 1980. Fred Figures finally, after some months after the shooting, is arrested for the crime.

"Now, that in broad strokes is what the evidence will show in this case. I'd ask you to listen carefully throughout the course of the trial to any and all witnesses in the trial. Keep an open mind throughout the trial and, at the conclusion of that evidence, and on the basis of that evidence, I'm going to ask each of you to find the Defendant guilty as charged."

McGuirl walked toward the jury box and was silent for a moment and then as if remembering his parochial school manners he added boyishly, "Thank you."

Before the defense attorney could begin his plea, Fred Figures was on his feet. "I want to talk."

Judge Davis gestured to his clerk, "Will you take the jury out for about ten minutes, please?" He turned to them. "I'm sorry for the interruption, ladies and gentlemen."

Once the twelve men and women had left, Davis, annoyed, looked at Figures. "Now that the jury is out and we have had an opening statement by the People, are you still interested in making your own opening statement?"

Figures said excitedly, "Yes sir," drawing out the last word.

Davis nodded. "I would very seriously love to let you make your own opening statement, but so far it sounds to me like the People have not even brought you into this case. It had nothing to do with drugs."

Figures broke in. "Say—"

Davis cut him off. "So far the People have not brought you into the drug scene. So far all they have brought you in is with a shot. That's all I've heard. And I think that your lawyer will do a much better job." Davis turned toward the defense attorney. "Do you intend to make an opening statement?"

Gonzalez, a trifle put off said, "Yes, it was my intention, your Honor."

"I'm going to let your lawyer make it," Judge Davis said firmly.

"That's your ruling?"

"That's my ruling, because I think you're going to hurt yourself. I've had more trials than you have. Look, Mr. Figures, I want to tell you something—"

"I'm talking to my lawyer."

Judge Davis leaned toward him. A determined look on his face, "I want you to know this, I don't care what you think about me. It doesn't make a difference, but you're going to get a fair trial, in spite of yourself, and don't forget it." Davis directed his next comments to Figures' attorney. "You want to put him back in and talk to him inside? I'd rather you talk to him inside."

"No."

"I don't want you to expose strategy here in front of me."

Gonzalez shook his head. "We are all right, your Honor."

Judge Davis said exasperately, "All right, bring the jury back in."

Gonzalez, the well-seasoned defendant's attorney, stepped forward with a slight flourish and began by quickly introducing himself and his client's case to the jury.

"Fred Figures is only asking you to listen to the evidence and evaluate the evidence. And at the end to give him a fair trial. Now that's a very simple concept and that's what he's asking for. The People of the State of New York, through Mr. McGuirl, has read off from the indictment the charges against Mr. Figures. And I think from our conversation before, you understand that the charges at this point are just what it says, they're charges. They're written down on paper. Nothing has been proven. And I'm asking you to be patient and to stay with this case and give both sides the kind of attention so that you will know where the evidence lies and where the fair trial will lie.

He straightened his stance and looked straight at the jurors one by one.

"And by the way, speaking of charges, when I say I represent the Defendant in this case, I can honestly state at this point, I don't represent anybody in this case that is dealing in drugs or charged with drugs. I'm strictly representing a Defendant in this case that's being charged with the things that Mr. McGuirl said; nor do I represent anybody that was on the street at 143rd Street, as was mentioned someone named Cleo. I only represent the man in this case, Fred Figures.

"Now, you've all given us your promise that you will recognize that Fred Figures, as he sits in court today as throughout this trial, is innocent until the People of the State of New York are able, if they're able, to prove him otherwise. We are very serious in having this jury look at the evidence and put Mr. McGuirl as Prosecutor to his proof, of proving the case beyond a reasonable doubt. It's a very serious protection that the Defendant is entitled to, beyond a reasonable doubt. That's what you're going to have to evaluate in the case.

"Now, my real reason for being here now is to tell you what the Defendant's position is. I think it was made clear to you what the People's position is. The Defendant's position here—first of all, to make it easier and lay out his position, he—his position will admit to you that he was present at the time that this happened."

He glanced at McGuirl and frowned.

"He'll admit to you that there was a man with a hammer over a woman in a threatening manner, whichever way Mr. McGuirl described it." McGuirl wiped a few beads of sweat off his forehead. "I think you'll find there was no dispute with that. Also, that there was a gun at a point in time in the Defendant's hand. Also that the trigger was pressured at a point of time and a shot was fired. However, it's the Defendant's contention in this case the under the circumstance of all these Smith brothers and other men in the neighborhood, and under the pressure of the situation, that the gun was fired under conditions of not only self-defense, concern of his own self, but concern of the girl's safety. So you must understand that these are—that's what's behind the Defense in this case."

He paused, looked at McGuirl and then back at the jurors.

"Now, you have heard the prosecutor's side of it, and you know the Defendant has something that should be related to you as to his theory. The theory is that a shot was fired and it was fired in defense of a lady and in self-defense. And admittedly there's no connection in this case, as far as I'm concerned, with narcotics' traffic. If 143rd Street is concerned with that, that's something else. That is not who has been indicted or charged here. It's this Defendant. We must, throughout this trial, evaluate evidence so his rights are protected. And I ask you to listen to the evidence and at the end to evaluate and deliberate based upon the fair concepts which the Court has mentioned to you and will mention to you again in more detail later.

"Thanks for your anticipated attention," Gonzalez went back to his seat.

With the opening arguments ended, the prosecutor called his first witness, Detective John Miller, who had been the arresting officer. He not only gave testimony as to the frustrating job of apprehending Figures, but also as to the continuous efforts of Rita Webb Smith and indeed that of her entire family to bring the case to court. Nowhere was their diligence more visible than as defense attorney Gonzalez attempted to cast doubt on Miller's testimony and instead fleshed out the portrait of the Smith's battle for justice.

Mr. Gonzalez stepped forward. "I'd like to go into the investigation that you undertook. You say it started on the night of the shooting."

"That's correct," Miller answered firmly.

Gonzalez tested, "And then you proceeded to do everything you could to solve this situation. Is that right?"

Miller did not take the bait. "Yes, sir."

Gonzalez fished. "Did you work alone or with someone else?"

"I worked with another partner," Miller said.

Gonzalez looked up searchingly. "As you went along doing this, you had another case you were working on too, is that right?"

"Yes, sir."

"And I think the testimony you gave us was that although the shooting took place in August, the Defendant was apprehended in February. Is that right?"

"That's correct, sir," the endlessly polite detective replied.

Gonzalez, still prodding, went on. "And throughout that time, you were using all the sources you could to find the Defendant. Is that right?"

"Time permitting, yes, sir."

"When you say—how did you refer to those people? Cooperative individuals?"

"That's correct, sir."

"Informants?"

Miller looked at him, despite his usual calm demeanor, a slight edge came into his voice. "That's your term sir."

Gonzalez didn't miss a beat. "You would utilize informants who you were looking for, that's what I would like to know."

Miller saw where he was headed. "Excuse me?"

Gonzalez pressed. "How did you communicate with the informants to let them know who you were looking for?"

"Well, sir, I interviewed persons who were arrested on a daily basis. If they were arrested in a certain area, various units knew I was interested in speaking to people in that area. And if the person had no objections to speaking to me, I sat down and spoke to him."

"When you spoke to them, you didn't go up to them and say, 'Can you find Fred Figures for me?' There was some other way you did it?"

"Yes, sir."

The judge interrupted. "You got two questions. I don't know what the—"

Gonzalez stepped more artfully. "I will rephrase it. When you approach someone, a cooperative individual, how did you tell him who you were looking for? I'm talking about in this case."

"I sat down and I tried to establish how well they knew the area, persons who are known to frequent the area, and I gave them a couple of names that I had in the investigation."

"Not Fred Figures, though, did you?"

"No, sir."

"Did you have pictures?"

"No, sir."

"And all this time, the seven months that you were investigating, were you in contact with the Smith family?"

"Yes, sir, I was."

"So that you had several interviews with them. Is that right?"

"All of them."

Gonzalez took a deep breath and drew out the names. "I am talking about Rita Smith, David Smith, Mark Smith and Peter Smith."

"That's correct, sir," Miller said looking about the courtroom.

Detective Miller's portrait of the activism of the Smith family was further amplified when Rita's youngest son, Peter, was cross-examined by Gonzalez the next day.

Gonzalez stepped forward. "Peter you were—you are sixteen now?"

"Yes, sir."

"And at the time of the occurrence, you were what, fourteen?"

"I was fifteen."

"Fifteen?"

"Yes."

"How high do you go? How tall are you?"

"I'm six-one."

"And would it be fair to say that at the time of this occurrence, you were close to six foot also? You mentioned something, I think you used the phrase, task force. Were you telling the Court and the Jury that you and your family belonged to some sort of team that was trying to do something?"

"No."

"What do you mean," Gonzalez asked perplexed?

"I was making reference to Manhattan North. And this was a police task force that would come in the event that they had any extra or larger crime problems in my neighborhood. So what we would do, was we organized what's called agency people. If somebody in the next building saw somebody selling drugs, he would call somebody—call the police. We all decided we would call the police, set up some type of correspondence between us."

"When you say task force, you are referring to police activities?"

"Right."

"That has nothing to do with your neighbors?"

"No."

"What about you and your family? You had something organized too, didn't you?"

"Yes, we did."

"And you were undertaking to do something with respect to the law, right?"

"All we would do is notify the police."

"Were you authorized by the police department to do this?"

"Well I can't say we were authorized. All I can say is, my mother was a member of the precinct council and her neighbors were members of the precinct council. And on numerous occasions, I'm sure the subject of drug sales came up, you know. And they all decided what they would do, would be, you know, to notify the police."

"Are any members of your family, to your knowledge, given any special training by the police department to enforce this?"

"No,"

"Were you?

"Not at the time."

"Were you supplied with any badges?"

"NO we weren't," Peter's voice was loud and clear.

"Any certificates?"

Peter nodded his head affirmatively. "Yes, we were."

Gonzalez looked at him surprised. "You were? Were you supplied with any guns or any equipment?"

"No guns, no equipment."

"But still, you were part of this group that was undertaking this project, is that right?'

"That's correct."

After a few more questions, Gonzalez ended his cross.

That night, as McGuirl reported the proceedings over the phone to Rita who had been barred as a spectator because she was a prospective witness, he said prophetically, "Look, I think you ought to be especially careful right now. Whatever good intentions the defense is claiming, we all know what this trial is really about."

"Drugs," Rita said disgustedly. "Nothing but trash-peddling drug dealers stinking up our streets."

Nodding in agreement McGuirl cut in, "But there are higher powers off the streets whose money supply you're cutting down and they won't like it or you."

"I know," Rita said quietly. "I understand."

But a few nights later when the phone rang about nine o'clock, Rita noted the strange European accent. It wasn't any of the people from her neighborhood.

The voice said, "Is this Rita Smith?"

She replied, "Yes."

He said, "I'm just calling to let you know there's a contract out on your life."

"Who are you?" she asked slowly.

He identified himself as Philip Gambino. She breathed in recognizing the infamous name.

"That sounds like the name of one of those Mafia people. I've heard that name before, Philip Gambino."

He said, "Oh really?" And went on, "Well, you don't sound too upset."

Rita replied. "Why should I be? When my time comes, I'll go like everybody else does." And then "Bam!" She hung up the phone.

But she was more than a little scared. She called the precinct saying, "I don't know whether to take it seriously or not, but I just got this call. The man was a well spoken white man who talked to me."

Pranzo, who had answered, spoke up. "Aw, Rita, it probably wasn't . . ." and then he caught himself, "but we'll keep extra people on your street just in case."

The night before David testified, Rita wished there'd been a lot more and closer.

Near 9 p.m., a series of blasts shattered the glass in her living room window. "This doesn't sound right," she said running from the bedroom. When she saw the debris, she screamed to her kids, "Hit the floor, hit the floor." Frightened, they complied. Crawling to the telephone, Rita dialed police headquarters. Twenty minutes later police appeared at her door. They told her eight shots had been fired, apparently from a nearby rooftop. They found one of the bullets. It was a 22-caliber.

"You're lucky they didn't hit any of you," Pranzo said, "or worse. Where's David?"

"I'm here." Shakily, he walked out of his bedroom.

"Are you alright?" Pranzo asked.

"Damned right I am," David said defiantly. "And I'll be there tomorrow morning. You can tell Figures for me I'll be early."

Rita smiled proudly at him, but tears sprung to her eyes.

12

The Trial Builds

*W*hen David Smith took the stand the next day friends and neighbors seated in the courtroom watched apprehensively.

McGuirl began to question David about Cleo and her activities on West 143rd Street. Then he moved to the day David had been shot.

"Do you recall where you were on August 17, 1979 in the afternoon?" McGuirl asked David.

"Yes," David replied, his eyes fastened on Fred Figures. "Took a shower and got dressed, and went out jogging."

"Do you remember where you run? If you do."

"Yeah, I run down Fifth Avenue."

Pinpointing the sequence McGuirl moved in. "What time did you get back from the run?"

"About 4:30."

David seemed hesitant. McGuirl didn't want the case hung up on insignificant factors. "Are you sure of the time?"

"No, I'm not sure of the time," David admitted.

McGuirl moved back. "Was it late afternoon?"

"Yeah."

"What were you wearing?"

"A sweatsuit."

"Could you describe that sweatsuit?"

"A sweat top and sweat pants."

Knowing that Figures might claim self-defense, McGuirl wanted to make clear David was unarmed. "Were there any pockets in the sweat top?"

"No."

"Any pockets in the sweat pants?"

"No."

"Was there any place where you could carry something?"

"My keys. I had to tie them onto the waistband."

McGuirl looked at Figures and then asked David, "You had to tie them onto something?"

"Yeah. I couldn't put them in nothing."

"Did you have anything else with you besides your keys?"

"No," David said firmly.

McGuirl nodded. "After you returned from running, where did you go?"

"To the Mother Nature Health Food Store."

"Where is that?" McGuirl continued.

"665 Lenox Avenue."

"What cross street on Lenox?"

"Depends on how you're crossing."

"What block is it by?"

"143rd Street and Lenox Avenue."

"Is that near your house?"

"That's up under my house."

Then McGuirl began to tie in other witnesses. "Did you see anyone you know there?"

"Yeah, I seen Aziz, my brother Peter, Ronald Shariff and the owner of the store Daoud Fawcett."

McGuirl paused for a moment. He had set time and place and now he was ready. "Could you tell the jury what happened that afternoon?"

"We was outside talking and we noticed Smoke."

"Who is Smoke?"

"Smoke is a drug peddler."

"Go ahead," McGuirl prompted him, "What did you see?"

"Smoke and Figures—I mean Fred Figures—," David's voice fell.

One of the jurors, a slight, balding man leaned forward. "I can't hear."

"Try to speak up," McGuirl said.

Judge Davis broke in. "Keep your voice up. The jurors can't hear."

McGuirl knew David was apprehensive. He nodded approvingly toward him. "Lean closer to the mike, if you have to. Do you recognize anyone in the courtroom today?"

David took a deep breath. "Yes."

"Could you point out the person you recognize?"

David was ready now, his voice firm. He stared at the

dcfendant. "I recognize Mr. Figures, sitting with his attorney over there." David paused and looked up. "And I recognize Cleo sitting in the back.

Heads turned. No one had noticed the usually swaggering Cleo unobtrusively sitting in the last row.

"The woman with the black leather jacket," David continued.

Judge Davis intervened. "Just walked out the door?"

David nodded. "Just walked out the door."

McGuirl couldn't suppress a smile but he kept going. "Directing your attention again to that afternoon, did you see Cleo that afternoon?"

"Yeah, I seen her," David nodded.

"And tell the jury what you saw."

Speaking quietly, rationally, David went on. "She was in the block. And when I was talking to Daoud and my brother, Peter, and Aziz, Daoud had a customer, he went inside to take care of the customer he had." He paused. "And I noticed Mark had Cleo in the collar with his right hand, and had a hammer in his left hand, and he pushed her up against the truck."

McGuirl digressed. "Was Mark working at that time?"

"Yes."

"What was he doing?"

"Electrical work."

"Did he have any tools?"

"Yeah, electricians have tools."

McGuirl blushed. He knew David must have been thinking damned fool college boy. "Had you seen him before you saw him with Cleo?"

"That day, no, not that I remember."

"Tell us what you saw. You said you saw Mark and Cleo."

"Yeah. And he was—he was taking the hammer and shaking it in her face talking to her, emphasizing he didn't want her there—"

Figures' attorney stood up and raised his hand. "It's not a responsive question."

Judge Davis scratched his head. "Let me hear the question please."

The question was reread.

The judge said to the witness. "Tell us what you saw."

David spoke up. "Mark was shaking the hammer in her face, moving his lips."

"Did you hear what was being said?" McGuirl asked slowly with trepidation hoping he wasn't going to get an answer he couldn't live with.

"No, I didn't."

McGuirl breathed a sigh of relief. "Where were Mark and Cleo?"

"They was on the cross-walk, right where he get up on the Avenue, and there is a truck parked that sells hamburgers and french fries. And he had her up against the truck."

"Was he holding her in any way?"

"He had her on the collar."

"Could you show with your hands what you saw?"

David closed his eyes for a moment then opened them wide. "I seen Mark, he had Cleo and the collar and the hammer in his hand, shaking the hammer in her face."

Judge David intervened. "You are indicating that hammer in his left hand, correct?"

David went on. "In his left hand and had her by the collar in his right hand."

"Where were Cleo's hands?" McGuirl asked.

"Cleo's hands were down, I think."

"When you say down, what do you mean?"

"By her side."

"And could you see if she was—could you see her lips moving?"

"Yeah, I seen her lips moving."

"Now, did you see when Mark first went over there?"

"Yes, I did. When he had the collar, when he came around the corner."

"And how long were Mark and Cleo talking until something else happened?" McGuirl queried.

"About thirty, maybe fifteen seconds, thirty seconds."

"Then did you see the Defendant that day?"

"Yes, I did," David said forcefully.

"Where was he?" McGuirl asked.

"He was sitting on the car with Smoke," David said decisively.

"Where was that?"

"On Lenox and 143rd."

Judge David queried. "What Avenue?"

David replied, "Lenox Avenue."

"What happened then?" McGuirl asked.

Tight lipped, David went on. "And I went, I seen Fred Figures moving toward my brother and I went over to intercept and talk to him, I told him that he didn't know what was going on, it was none of his business. And he told me it was none of my business. And we started pushing and shoving, and I started seeing him reach into his pants and I hit him."

McGuirl interrupted. "You say you saw him reaching in his pants?"

"His belt buckle."

"Belt buckle?" McGuirl repeated.

"Yes." David shook his head affirmatively. "He pulled his jacket up with his left hand."

"What did you do?"

"He ran back then."

"Did you hit him at some point?"

For the first time David smiled. "Yeah, I hit him in the jaw."

"What happened after you hit him in the jaw?" McGuirl asked in a businesslike tone.

"He ran back," David said serious again.

"How far?"

"About ten feet."

David was looking away. McGuirl drew him back. "What happened then?"

David looked up aware that all eyes were focused on him. He spoke intently. "Then he pulled out a pistol and said 'Mother Fucker, I'm going to kill you.'"

McGuirl let the remark sink in then he said, "Where did he pull the pistol from?"

"In the middle of his pants."

"And once he pulled the pistol out. What did he do with it?"

"He brung it up high."

"Was it pointing towards anything?"

David nodded. "Pointing towards my head."

"And what position—what were your positions, Mr. Figures position and your position, with regard to each other?"

"We was face on."

The judge cleared up any obscurity. "Meaning face to face?"

David said, "Face to face."

McGuirl went on. "When he pulled out that gun and he put—pointed it towards you, what did you do?'

"I tried to move out of the way. I tried to turn and run."

"What happened?"

"I felt something hit me in my jaw. And as I turned, I heard a shot."

"Then what happened."

"Then I ran off. Tried to catch the cab and go to the hospital. Then I stopped on 141st Street and checked and felt my jaw."

"What did you find?" McGuirl asked coolly.

"Oh, my teeth. I was spitting out my teeth. And I thought half my jaw was gone."

Gonzalez rose. "Move to strike as not responsive."

The judge interrupted. "What did he find?"

Gonzalez replied, "He said 'I thought.'"

Judge Davis considered the request for a moment before saying, "Strike that part. He was spitting out his teeth."

McGuirl prompted. "Were you bleeding?"

"Yes I was."

"Do you know if you spit out anything else besides your teeth?"

"A bullet," David replied.

"What did you do then?"

"I went to the hospital."

"And what happened at the hospital?"

"They put me on the table and gave me some needles. And the doctor came in and started to work on my mouth."

David's strong, clear testimony seemed to give others added courage. And when his friend, Abdel Aziz, testified, although he was obviously nervous, he, too, was forthright just as he had promised Rita on the night David had been shot.

"Mr. Aziz, try to keep your voice up—," McGuirl implored him.

Judge Davis said, "Spell the middle name."

Aziz did in a quiet, firm voice. "A-B-D-E-L."

McGuirl frowned. "Mr. Aziz, have you ever been arrested or convicted of any crime?"

"Yes, sir, I have," Aziz said soberly.

McGuirl prompted him. "Could you tell the Jury about that?"

"When I was younger, I was born in Florida, and I came up to New York at the age of thirteen. And prior to coming here, I got into some trouble with the law, and I got arrested for receiving stolen property. And I did—I got three years probation. And in 1974, I was arrested also. And in between those times, I had gotten in trouble with the law. In 1974, I got into some trouble with the law, and it was dismissed, the charge was dismissed. And I used drugs also."

McGuirl wanted it all out in the open. "What type of drugs, prior to 1974, did you use?"

"Heroin," Aziz said contritely.

"How long did you use heroin prior to 1974?"

"About three years."

"Now, in 1974, you had been arrested, you had been

convicted a few times, you were using heroin. What happened in 1974?"

Aziz looked more confident now as he explained, "Afterwards, it being in '74, that was the last arrest. I was working for West Harlem Community Management. And I was coming out of an apartment doing some work, and the police officer was looking for someone who had robbed a restaurant, and I was in the hallway, and they grabbed me. And I resisted them and the took me to the precinct and they charged me with resisting arrest and possession of a weapon.

"But the charge wasn't proven, it wasn't so, it was dismissed.

"And prior to that, I began to get—come out into the community and get involved in community activities. Registering voters, registrations and various community programs."

Aziz began to visibly relax.

"And I began to go to school to try to complete my education. And I began to see the community fall, I was tired of it, so as a result, I did—I got involved into the community and I was sick of it. I was sick of drugs, sick of seeing the community fall down. I was sick of seeing people selling drugs in the community and basically I was sick of my conditions and the conditions of the people that was around me."

His voiced firmed toward the end.

"So I started to get involved into the community activities. And what had happened is that I would come out into the community and I would see people—"

Gonzalez stepped in. "You Honor, I move to strike. I think he's gone way beyond the response."

186

Judge Davis contemplated. "Well, the only way I would strike it—you can't listen to the whole thing and you don't like it. I will stop him at this point."

McGuirl picked up the discussion. "Mr. Aziz, until 1974, at some point you were using heroin, you had some conflict with the law. Was 1974 the last time you had a conflict with the law?"

"Yes, sir," Aziz said, nodding his head.

"What about heroin. Are you using heroin now?"

"No, sir," Aziz said.

"When did you stop using heroin?"

" '72. Around '72."

"Are you employed now?"

"Yes, sir."

"How old are you?"

"I'm thirty-three."

"Where are you employed now?"

"I work at West Harlem, the same job I had in '74. I still have the same job. And I work various jobs. And I volunteer. I do a lot of volunteer work at Sister Clare Mohammed Elementary second school. I teach physical education to children, work with the Boy Scouts and I write plays and songs and various positive programs that they put on."

"What is the West Harlem Corporation you have spoken of? What is it?"

"It's a community management program. What they do is they take buildings and they go down to the city and they get these building and they rehab them."

"What kind of buildings?"

"Buildings that have been abandoned by landlords. Buildings the city has taken over."

"Have you ever done any work in the prisons?"

"Beg your pardon."

"Have you ever done any work in the prisons?"

"Yes, sir."

"Tell the Jury about that."

"I worked with a program called KAPP Community Assistance Prison Project. And I go up to Sing Sing and various prisons. I go in because I write—I write plays and skits dealing with the problems that we're having in the community in order to try to solve a lot of problems that we have. Since I've been a problem myself, I feel—,"

Gonzalez raised his hand. "Objection. Move to strike."

Judge Davis looked up. "Mr. Aziz, please try to stick to a response to the questions without going too far afield. If the answer calls for a yes, just give the answer; if the answer calls for a no; if anything else, just answer that and nothing else. Go ahead."

"Mr. Aziz, let me direct your attention to August 17, 1979. On that day, did you know any people by the name of Smith?"

"Yes, sir."

"And could you tell us what Smiths you know and how you know them."

Aziz smiled. "I know Ms. Rita Smith, David Smith, Peter Smith, Mark; I know the whole family, all of them. I can name them all."

McGuirl smiled back. "How did you get to know them?"

"We usually—in the evenings usually come around—I worked at Fish and Burger Restaurant. I worked there for about three years, and I got to know them in coming into the restaurant. And I saw the activities that Mrs. Smith was creating in the block, in the neighborhood, in trying to clean the neighborhood up."

"What kind of activities?"

"As far as housing and fighting against the drug pushing in the community and stuff like that. So I became familiar with them. I like it there because, me being from that background, I wanted to get involved in that."

"Were you present on 143rd Street near Lenox on August 17, 1979?"

"Yes, sir."

"And about what time did you go there?"

"I was there early, around—it was after three o'clock."

"How long were you there?"

"I was there a long time. We were there—I can't say exactly how long it was, but—,"

McGuirl broke in. "What were you doing?"

"We were standing around discussing different programs we were trying to start, cleaning the streets, keeping the street clean and about the conditions of the streets."

"Who was there?"

"David, Peter, myself and there were about four other people that were there, Daoud, Shariff, other people that were there."

McGuirl asked a few more questions about the scene and then moved to the incident with Fred Figures.

Aziz spoke slowly, clearly. "David had moved back and he lunged towards David and shot David here, right here." Aziz gestured.

"Did he point the pistol?" McGuirl asked feelingly.

"Yes he did." Aziz looked over at his friend and then back at the prosecuter.

"Where did he point it?" McGuirl prodded.

Aziz sighed heavily. "Towards his head."

"Do you know if anything was said?"

"The only thing that I heard him say was to leave her alone and David said mind your own business."

"And did you see the gun fired?"

"Yes, I saw when he shot."

"Do you know if anything was said at that time?"

"I wasn't aware of anything that was said."

"What happened then after the gun was fired?"

"After he shot David, David jumped back and he ran. David ran towards Harlem Hospital."

When Aziz finished his testimony, Leland Robinson, the oral and maxillo facial surgeon who had treated David at Harlem Hospital, took the stand to describe David's wounds. As Robinson spoke, the jury appeared to McGuirl to be nodding sympathetically, McGuirl told Rita later that night. He didn't tell her he had been glad she hadn't been there to hear her son's wounds and the danger to him described so graphically.

"David Smith is a twenty-year-old black male. At the time I saw him, he was alert, co-operative. His jaw was, what appeared initially, was a laceration on his left jaw, a stellar type of laceration."

Davis interrupted. "Stellar means it was in a star shape?"

Doctor Robinson said, "A star-shaped type of laceration on the left chin. Looking inside his lip, on the left side of his face, I saw that the laceration was a through laceration. In other words, it came through the outside of his mouth through into the inside of his mouth and hit his mandible. His mandible being, which you saw, the lower jaw. I saw that there was a portion that bears the teeth of the bone was completely shattered. There was a laceration in the floor of his mouth and there was a laceration of his tongue."

"Doctor," McGuirl interrupted, "could you point on your own person to where the surface wound, the outside wound on David Smith's face was?"

"It came right about here," the doctor said indicating the region on his own face.

"Indicating a spot—"

Judge Davis jumped in. "The lower left jaw, just under the lip."

Robinson nodded. "Right."

"Doctor, you stated your initial suspicion was that it was a laceration."

"It appeared to be a laceration."

"And did you conduct further examination of the wound?"

"On further examination, internally, inside the mouth I saw fragments of bone and soft tissue. The tissue was avulused, that means it was completely destroyed. I saw a piece of heavy-type metal in the area of this large abyss portion of the mandible."

"Would your form an opinion as to how that wound was caused?"

"Gun, a missile, bullet."

"The wound was consistent with that caused by a gunshot?"

"Yes." The doctor nodded.

"And, Doctor, you described the point of entry as being

below on the left side of the jaw. Where was the next, where was the line of damage?"

"The line of damage was, as I mentioned before, through the cheek, the left chin. The missile shattered the mandible in that area. The interior, the superior border of the mandible was shattered, to the mandible and into the floor of the mouth and across the tongue. That was the path of the bullet."

"In other words, it would go to this point that you described, go into what we commonly call the inside of the mouth, the floor of the mouth."

"Yes."

"And what was the course of treatment for David Smith?"

"The course of treatment was to check his vital signs to see if he was stable; to see if there was any respiratory distress. Once that was attained, ascertained that he was stable, the lacerations in this mouth were closed, repaired, sutured, that is."

"Was David Smith admitted to the hospital?"

"Yes, he was admitted to the ward."

Later, McGuirl asked the doctor, "Doctor, can a wound caused by a missile to that area of the body cause death?"

The doctor looked up soberly and pondered the question for a moment. "Yes."

Quickly Gonzalez spoke up. "Objection. Speculation."

Judge Davis, loudly announced, "Overruled."

The last of the Smith family to testify was Rita's second son, Mark, whose telling description of what his street was now like filled the courtroom.

"Gradually you had more addicts coming into the neighborhood. Started setting fires to buildings, burned them down so they have some place to shoot the drugs, and it continued like this for a while and moved down further and further, up until '79, where it was, I say at its peak, really worse. And the drug dealers, they began to come into the open, whereas before they were dealing behind closed doors where you wouldn't be able to see them; and they started coming into the open."

"What would you actually see?"

"You would see them make the transaction of drugs. You see money going into their hands and you see drugs going to whoever was buying it, into their hands."

"What happened?"

"Well, that continued, and then along with that, they started, you know, shooting, shooting each other over little simple things. If you were to sell maybe some drugs to an addict who used to buy from somebody else, and this guy caught you, he may shoot you for that, and it was a regular thing for them to have shoot-outs on that block and more buildings began to burn down and the people just started to move out, and pretty soon you had almost five, I'd say about five buildings that were just vacant, just in one summer."

"What did you do about this, if anything?"

"Well, I tried to avoid them, you know, I wouldn't walk up the block. I more or less—my building was on the corner, so I'd like go around. I tried not to walk up that block, to try and prevent from getting shot or anything else, and I would stay in the house a lot. I wouldn't, you know, I wouldn't frequent the area. I'd go somewhere else and I'd, you know, watch out for my younger brother and sisters. I watched out for them."

"Did there come a time when you began to speak to some of the people in the narcotics traffic in the block?"

"Yes."

"Tell the Jury about that."

"This was during 1979. It started about in the winter of 1979 when they started to come in front of the building and on the stoop itself, and they would sell the drugs right on this stoop and if I caught them, I would ask them to move. I asked them not to bring that over here because of the fact that it was a private building, it's privately owned and we had kids coming in and out of the building. And they would do it in front of the kids. They would do it—the kids could be standing next to them and they do it there. If they got into a situation where they have to shoot someone, they do it in front of the kids. It really meant nothing to them."

As the picture of West 143rd Street's worsening condition and drug dealers like Fred Figures' participation in that decline grew sharper, Fred was growing visibly edgy. Several times he began to rise to his feet. Putting a hand on Figures' shoulder, Gonzalez tried to quiet him. Figures' pushed him away and his annoyance at being silenced erupted.

"I'm tired of this, I can't get no type of cooperation with me and my lawyer. We have been beefing ever since the beginning of this trial. Now we are still beefing."

Gonzalez said, half tongue-in-cheek. "I'm not beefing," drawing out the first word.

The judge, picking up Gonzalez's joking mood, broke in. "Before the beefing is finished or while you are beefing, I want you to sit tight for a minute. I have a comment. I was told last night that there was this woman, Cleo, out in the corridor. She was not called by the defense. I assume you didn't want to call her, Mr. Gonzalez. Is that correct?"

Gonzalez put his forefinger on his temple. "I discussed that thoroughly with the defendant and I was told that there was no witness to be produced. Mr. Figures preferred not to put her on the stand."

Judge Davis nodded. "I just want to make sure before we start that there was not an accidental omission."

Gonzalez gestured. "We discussed it thoroughly over a period of many days, actually, your Honor."

Judge Davis went on. "So we have summations and charge. Let me tell you what the charge is going to be. We have discussed it once, but before summation and charge, I am going to tell you the general way the charge will be. First, do you have any requests? Other side have any requests?"

Gonzalez replied, "Not at this time, your Honor."

Judge Davis announced, "Now, as far as the indictment is concerned, the jury will be given all the counts."

He went on to delineate just what the counts consisted of for which Gonzalez said, "Thank you."

The McGuirl's voice cut in, "Part of your justification charge includes a statement of deadly physical force?"

Judge Davis looked him in the eye. "Yes. It is in the statute. Okay, we are ready to start? Let's not have any interruptions, please, during summation."

Despite the judge's instructions to the lawyers to begin to sum up quickly, Fred Figures again broke in. "May I have a word with my lawyer before summation?"

Judge Davis said exasperatedly, "Go ahead."

Figures persisted. "Can I speak with him in the back, please?"

Judge Davis, visibly annoyed now, breathed in. "You know, it is already eleven o'clock."

Gonzalez looked at his watch. "I am prepared to go ahead with summation based on the evidence in this trial. I don't need any suggestions from the defendant with respect to the preparation of the summation. I've been an attorney almost thirty years. I have tried several homicide cases and thousands of trials. I can comment on the evidence without any advice from this defendant."

Judge Davis tried to keep his voice level. "Now Mr. Figures, the only thing we have today is the summation, which means he is going to review the evidence for the jury and ask them to draw certain conclusions and he will make a fair comment. That's all he is entitled to do today, but you have in mind not something that he might have in mind, and I would prefer to rely on his ability to sum up rather than your instructions to him as to how he is to sum up."

Figures was boiling. "Yesterday in this courtroom I seen his ability to disregard the evidence that shows that there's been discrepancy between testimony, and that the complainant and all his witnesses that got on the stand and testified to and from the information, that I was the individual selling drugs there and that Cleo was not involved, and they got on the stand and testified to it, But the fact was that Cleo was the one that was selling drugs."

Judge Davis said, "Mr. Figures, I would tell you right now that the jury is going to be told that the People in the case have no evidence indicating that you were selling drugs on 143rd Street. The jury will be so charged, so don't get excited about it.

"What about the information that I produced?"

"The jury can draw any inference they want from that," Judge Davis said firmly and closed the matter.

13

The Trial Ends

---

*O*n the sun speckled May morning of the last day of testimony Judge David began, "Good morning, members of the jury. We will now have summation and charges."

With that Gonzalez, with a tight lipped smile, stepped forward and began his final argument.

"May it please the Court, Madam Forelady, Mr. Mc-Guirl, ladies and gentlemen of the jury, as what was promised at the outset, this is the opportunity for counsel to come back to you and to comment on the evidence that you've seen and the evidence that you've heard, when you're doing your deliberations and it is only that, it is only counsel's comments. We, in this system, we have here, we rely heavily on the memories and the observations and the conclusion of the members of our community who are the jury. I asked you at the outset for certain assurances. I think I asked that probably throughout all the jury selection and everybody seemed conscientious, everybody seemed to give us those assurances. Of course, the very obvious assurances being that it was your intention that this defendant be given a fair trial throughout and I am convinced that is your intention."

After he had expanded on that statement Gonzalez turned to another subject.

"I think it is obvious, I mentioned at the outset of this case I am not defending a narcotics case, I am not defending narcotics traffic at 143rd Street or anywhere else. I find that, I am sure you do, narcotics traffic is distasteful in our community. I cannot personally condone the use of words that come across this witness stand. I am sure many of you feel the same way, so I don't want you to think that in any way I endorse the use of those words at random.

"When a bullet is fired and someone is shot, it is something we have to take seriously. I don't condone that and I am sure you don't. I am sure you know where we stand at the outset. This is not my position to condone any kind of crimes. That would be distasteful to the members of the community." He regarded the jury levelly with tired, brown eyes.

"The evidence in this trial are some police complaint records, basically follow-up reports where police officers took interviews from certain people, and we would like the jury to have as much information as possible. These have been put into evidence and you have an opportunity to read the interviews that were given, but on behalf of the defendant I think it should be mentioned to you that certain things appear inconsistent with all the testimony. For instance, you will notice, if you read those carefully, that there is no mention in the complaint reports about Mark Smith chasing a woman with a hammer in a moving position. You notice that is completely left out of the interview reports.

"Now, you will know from the police officers who testified and also from Mark Smith that these interviews are considered rather informational and the information should be accurate and complete. You'll also notice that one of these exhibits, one of these complaint reports, there is a paragraph that refers to an input by Rita Smith, who is the mother of these boys, and who, there is no question, had a very active interest in getting things done, and we bring that to you because we'd like you to keep it in the back of your mind, the motives of Rita Smith and the Smith family, their interest in this case and how they submitted their information to the police department, and that's why those two reports are in evidence without any objection by the defendant, because the defendant wants you to read as much information from written statements that you can in addition to the oral testimony."

Gonzalez looked sympathetically at the jury and nodded.

"Now, you really have enough to do listening to a trial full of evidence and then going and deliberating on a couple of days of evidence and then coming to a crucial decision at the end, so anything that we can do at this point to narrow all your considerations, I like to do and I like to say very simply how obviously there are certain things that there are no issue about. This isn't the kind of case where the defendant is trying to convince you he wasn't there. He was there and there seems to be no doubt about that. He was there, the gun was there, the gun was in his hand, the trigger on that gun was activated. All these things were present. Obviously we don't have to talk or sit around and talk about them anymore and also certain words were uttered. It seems that all the witnesses say that. Also, very obviously in this case, the witnesses were more or less consistent on the stand about this, is that Mark Smith, who you saw only yesterday, was chasing after the woman with a hammer raised in his hand, and was cursing at her. He admits to that, so it is an obvious thing, it certainly is, this moving hammer; whether he was moving, twisting or moving this way, he admits that he was moving the hammer, so those things are all pretty obvious. I try to make a point out of the fact that this atmosphere, and I will talk more about it again, up at 143rd and Lenox on that particular evening, in this atmosphere, a woman was being chased by Mark Smith and nobody, of all these people that were around, they all had different interests, no doubt about it, but nobody was intervening to stop Mark Smith from hitting her or menacing her with a hammer, including Mark Smith's brother. There was no reason why these brothers couldn't have intervened and told him to cool it, but none of them offered to do that."

He swallowed hard. "Now, these are men, all these Smith boys testified, these are men that told you about their sincere, conscientious interest about, first of all, their block and secondly, about the people they worried about, what happens to people, they say. Now something was really happening to this women, Cleo, and nobody really worried except the defendant, Fred Figures."

Gonzalez spoke for a while about the active participation of the Smith family in ridding the block of dope dealers and whether it went beyond the law. Then he said, "This situation, that evening, the defendant was present and he was more or less alone, practically alone. I heard some testimony that he was in the company of another person, but when you put that up against a family plus their friends who customarily met at that store and they were, most of them were present, there is more to this atmosphere than a one-on-one situation. The defendant Fred Figures was in an atmosphere where there were many people around him and there is no indication whether any of them or more than one were friendly to him at this time.

"I ask you to observe a vital element in this case. It came from the lips of Mark Smith and I think by the way, take a lot of what Mark Smith said on the stand was quite intent to tell the truth; Mark Smith told you a time frame."

Gonzalez narrowed his eyes and spun out Fred Figure's theory of the shooting.

"Quickly, within that time frame, is resentment on Mark's part, a reaction on his part, chasing, cursing, and the movement of the hammer. Within that same time, David appears from someplace, from the side or the rear of the defendant, Fred Figures, and they face each other and there is a punch. Now this punch comes—if you see the size of Fred Figures—it comes from David Smith, six feet, two hundred twenty pounds. Now, maybe in a one-on-one situation, maybe Fred Figures might have held his own for a while, or tried to hold, I don't know, but this is not a one-on-one situation. There is Mark Smith with a hammer, the other Smith brothers are behind or—everyone is there and the punch takes place and there was a shot fired. The use of the language, I don't intend to repeat it. I don't see any need for the use of the language. At that point it fits into the pattern, under pressure, intimidating atmosphere on the street by a street person. We might not condone it, but I don't know if we should be overshocked with it, but what you have to figure is the reaction of Fred Figures under all these circumstances, everybody around him, the man in front of him, the punch at him and everything else. I have heard in less intimidating circumstances like riding a city bus, I heard young men use that same language. I comment to myself that I thought it was unnecessary, but with a reaction I think it should be almost understandable that this thing, the hammer and I heard people say, 'I'll kill you, I'll kill you', a quick reaction when somebody annoys them. There is more than that to this. It was an intimidating circumstance with a person carrying a hammer, what was happening with the woman, the danger, a punch coming from David Smith and all of these big guys behind him and also being without too much support. These are the things I ask you to keep in mind. Don't ever lose sight of that for one minute, the time frame and all the things that happened, and now you're in the spotlight and in the shoes of the defendant, Fred Figures. What are you doing? All of this talk, this evaluating, all the reaction and under all the circumstances you are evaluating whether this reaction was proper. You probably know that I speak first at this time. It is a reverse order from what we did at the beginning of the trial, but I also speak for the last time on behalf of the defendant."

As he went on, Gonzalez was trying to elicit sympathy

for Figures' lack of education and poverty. "For one thing, he doesn't get an opportunity to tell you these things. I try to put them all together, sum them up, try to get the important ones for you, and you will find that probably I have missed a couple of points. You might wonder why I didn't mention them. It will be taken care of by the memory of the jurors." In addition, he complimented their intelligence.

"After I speak, the District Attorney and, by the way, I can afford to come up here and hit the highlights and be brief and tell you what I think are the important things because the defendant does not have an obligation in this case to prove himself innocent, and I, as his attorney, I don't have an obligation to prove him innocent. However, after I speak the District Attorney, who has a more complete obligation to prove guilt beyond a reasonable doubt, will cover every small facet in this case and he will cover everything he thinks you should be thinking of. I will not have an opportunity to rebut or come back again, so I have to rely on highlighting all the high spots now.

Aware that he was reaching rugged ground, Gonzalez stopped and was silent for a few minutes. Then he tried a new tactic to scale the rough terrain.

"The defendant's position in this case is that under the pressures and the atmosphere, the intimidating atmosphere, under the things that happened that night, the punch, under the fact that Cleo, the woman, was in danger to the defendant's mind, and observation; that she was in danger and all of this was happening in one minute, that the defendant was justified in the reaction, the act that he did in backing up, protecting himself, in self-defense and also his involvement in the whole thing was a part of an attempt to come to the defense of a woman in danger."

Gonzalez could now see signs of consternation among the jury members. He looked like he had anticipated the agitated reaction but he continued, his voice strong and clear, carefully, tediously making every point he could.

"Now, that is the defense of this defendant, that he was justified in his reaction because of the danger of the woman and because of the danger to himself and you are the ones that are going to have to judge that.

"Now, based on all this evidence and based on all this thinking, I am trying to review with you, I expect that on behalf of this defendant that you will bring in a verdict, after due deliberations with your peers here, of acquittal of Fred Figures, and I thank you for your attention." Gonzalez sat down.

Bob McGuirl, looking clean cut and boyish in a blue suit, stepped forward gingerly. His well thought out strategy belied his naive appearance.

"May it please the Court, you Honor, Justice Davis, Counsel, Madam Forelady and ladies and gentlemen of the jury, before I begin my summation, I want you to think about something. This takes place at 143rd Street between Seventh and Lenox Avenues. That is Harlem. So what? Harlem can be a dangerous place, particularly for a narcotics dealer. What does a narcotics dealer have on him? Money, through transactions, and drug; work money. Who is that narcotics dealer meeting with all the time? Heroin addicts. Does a narcotics dealer have to be well-known to sell drugs? Certainly people like to know who he is. Common knowledge that he is a dealer, that he should have money, he or she should have money and should have drugs worth money on them. Well, like every other community, there are robbers in Harlem, there are muggers in Harlem. And who is a good target for robbery? There is no robbery in this case, understand that. Just talking to you about it. Who is a good target? Who can't complain to the police? Who does not have, because of what they're doing, protection of the police? Who can rob who can't complain to the police? Well, you know the answer, the narcotics dealer. And of all narcotics dealers, if you are dealing around 143rd Street back in the summer of 1979, you had an addition to that problem and the problem was a multiple problem; David Smith, Mark Smith, people like the Smiths; people like Edward Zeiss who was a problem to you for interfering with your God-given rights to deal with heroin in the streets. So, you had two problems. You had the one of having a large amount of money and narcotics and no protection from the police, no protection from the muggers, and you had the other problem with the Smiths constantly harassing and annoying if you are a narcotics dealer, making life very difficult for you, calling the police, going down basically and bothering you when you are trying to just deal with heroin. So what do you need? You can't get protection from the police. You need protection."

Gonzalez held up his hand. "I object to this unfair comment on the evidence. There has been no evidence along this line."

Judge Davis looked puzzled. "About what?"

Gonzalez replied, "Protection coming from any area with respect to narcotics."

Davis shook his head. "There has been testimony, I do not see how it relates to this defendant. The jury will be charged that the testimony, the drugs in the street does not indicate this defendant, but I can understand what he is talking about. Go ahead."

McGuirl continued, his voice rising forcefully, "I am asking you to consider this. Just use your own common sense, and some of you are from the area, from the community. Some of you are from elsewhere. Just use common sense when you think about this. You need protection, and what kind of protection do you need, a man with fists? What is a man with fists going to do with an armed robber, yell at him? How about a man with a knife? Can't use a knife unless you are close to someone, really, and if the robber, whoever it is, has a gun, you are out of luck. What do you need? You need a man with a gun, and where does he have to be, five blocks away? No, he's got to be near you.

"Now, I'd like to thank you all for your time and your attention throughout the course of this trial. It is your participation as jurors that enables our jury system to work and I make one further comment about the jury system. The whole rationale behind the jury system is to have a jury of peers, jury of people from the community and all of you are people from the community. You are not from the Bronx, you are not from Queens, you are not from Jersey, you are all from Manhattan and this is your town and this is your community, and for that reason you sit and you judge. No one else from someplace else. You are the community. You judge this case. And for that I thank you all for your participation.

"Now, you heard Mr. Gonzalez. What does he say? Well, there is no dispute over the defendant being there. There was no dispute over the shooting. Well, what is the only thing left the defendant could possible raise? There has been an attempt to be raised here justification or what some people might call self-defense. So it has been raised, so let us deal with it, think about it. What is justification?

Well, as his Honor will tell you specifically what justification is as defined in the law, and that's the instructions you should follow to a "T" when you boil it down, you will probably find it is going to come in accord with your own ideals of what is right, what is permissible to defend yourself and what is not. But his Honor will tell you more about it."

McGuirl's message was plain, unequivocal.

"Justified for what? Justified for survival is what it is really coming down to, and you got a conflict here and it has been attempted to be pointed out to you as Fred Figures' struggle, survival. But you sit down and you think about this case, you think about the evidence in this case, and that conflict that has been going on more or less for a while between the narcotics dealers on that block and the people like the Smiths. You think about whose struggle for survival this is, whose block it is, who lives there, who's really the person struggling for surviving here, are the people who dug in, didn't move off the block and who fought to survive there. I think you will know the answer to that. I think when you think about what the Smiths were doing, the people on that block were doing, a couple of things will come to mind." McGuirl shrugged and paused. Then he shook his head emphatically.

"One, even though it has been cross-examined about, talking to a narcotics dealer, asking him to move off that block, there is nothing illegal about that. There was nothing wrong with that, and that's where you start, if you've got the nerve to go down there and do that. Remember, that's what they were doing. This is their community. Each one of you will go home to your homes tonight, and when you walk into your home tonight, think about when they walked into their homes back in August. Think about your doorstep, your block, decks going back and forth, the money going back and forth, the shootings, fires in the building. You know how you feel about your residence. Each of you understands how the Smiths may have felt about theirs. Two seven-year-old twins. Do you think you understand how the Smiths might feel about this? Why they might go out and stop it?

"Think about how they did try to stop it. They went out and tried calling the police. How effective is that going to be? Frequently? How frequent is that going to be? Police can only do so much. Beyond that, what else did they do? They went down and spoke to the people, and you recall at no point, there was no violence, no bats, guns or knives to take these dealers off the block. So you are getting into a mess yourself. You're trying everything to get them off the block and that is what was happening at this point.

"Was it well known? Of course it was well known. A lot of dealers did move on the block. Was it well known to this woman named Cleo? Certainly. Mark Smith spoke to her on several occasions. Did the Smiths make any attempt to hide what they were doing? Of course not. Did they make every attempt to make it known that they didn't want drug deal- ers on the block? Yes, they did. Common knowledge. And it had an effect on the narcotics traffic to a degree," McGuirl insisted firmly.

"Everybody knew it, particularly Cleo knew it. Cleo had some problems on that block. She used to leave and she would come back. She was asked to leave and she would come back, and these Smiths were just messing up the whole business. They were just causing her a lot of hassles. Who wants to buy from her? Somebody yelling, 'I'm going to call the cops'—it's no good. Well, she'd been there before on that block. There was something different about August 17th."

He went on to describe the scene as the witnesses saw it.

Then McGuirl said, "Now, after these problems, Cleo had Fred Figures appear on the block and Fred Figures was armed with a gun and Fred Figures is right in the vicinity of Cleo and 'Smoke', and who is Smoke? You don't recall? Smoke is another narcotics dealer. So, now, on the 17th, things are a little different. Now Fred Figures is here and Fred Figures is armed and Fred Figures is right near where she is dealing with Smoke and another dealer.

He was carefully building the scene. "Now the Smiths come out. They don't know this. They've never seen Figures before. You get a little different perspective of what is going to happen. Something I should mention. You listened to the Smiths, you listened to all the witnesses. You should have noticed at some point, you know, David didn't tell it exactly the same way as Peter. Didn't Mark say he wasn't standing there talking with him, a couple of things like that? And you will notice it is not exactly the same. Well, think about it. Why isn't it exactly the same? It has been over a year and a half. What happens in a year and a half when you look at the same event? Well, you remember the important facts and each of them remembered the important facts."

McGuirl fleshed out the details further.

"Well, before we go any further, one of the charges in the indictment is possession of a loaded gun outside your home or place of business. Before anything happens on August 17th, don't you know, right now, each one of you, Fred Figures was in possession of a loaded gun outside his home or place of business on that day. Is that not clear? Is there any dispute over that? That tells you he is guilty of the fourth count of the indictment before we even start. What happens, all the witnesses saw the gun. He had a bullet, lead fragments. No question it was operable, it was an operable firearm and it also tells you that Fred Figures was there, he was armed, illegally armed. Now, for what purpose had Fred Figures come to that block? He was never seen there before, never visited them before. Let's see what happened, why Fred Figures was there.

He had reached the crisis point. "Mark Smith sees Cleo and Mark Smith has his electrician's tools and he got a hammer, and Mark Smith runs over and he grabs Cleo. Now he had the hammer with him, and all the witnesses have told you that he had the hammer up. There is no question about that. I ask you, all right, think about it. What does it mean? First blush—well, it sounds like—what does it mean about what happened?

"What was the testimony? Cleo had dealt with Mark before. No violence before. He wasn't going to hurt her. Did Cleo know this? They knew from past dealing with these people that they did not use violence. Where are the hands? I am coming back with a knife. Up go your hands. I am pointing a gun at you. Up go your hands. Where were Cleo's hands? By her side."

McGuirl began to stride back and forth making stinging points as he walked.

"I come to you with a knife. What do you yell? 'Help, help!' What was Cleo doing? Arguing. Oh sure, Mark was screaming at her, yelling at her. No question about that. But she is yelling back. What does that tell you? How afraid was she? She is afraid, that she can argue back with this guy? What does it tell anyone who is looking?

"Sure, you got a dispute here, some kind of dispute and everyone in the neighborhood knows what the Smiths are here for and what the dispute is about. There is no threat of immediate danger to her. Mark Smith didn't hit her in the head with the hammer. It is up there. He is holding her, yes, but her hand is down and she is yelling back at him.

"Was it a wise idea to bring over the hammer? No. But you're getting the truth and that's the way it happens. What does it mean? Well, what else do you know? . . . Cleo is not in danger of the hammer. What is she in danger of? She in is danger of losing her business once again, and Smith, whatever you want to call it, is messing it up again. That is what she is in danger of, being kicked off the block again for dealing in narcotics."

He stopped and looked straight at the jury expectantly.

"So what does the defendant do? He gets off the car. He begins to walk over, and what happens? David Smith is there. What does David Smith see? He sees this defendant sitting with Smoke and another dealer, and he sees Cleo. What does he do? He goes over and interrupts him. What is he wearing? Could David Smith be armed? What is he wearing? He is wearing sweatpants. Remember, this is August. This is the hottest part of the summer. He is wearing a sweatshirt. Does he have anything in his hands? No. "He comes over and stops Fred Figures and what does he say to him? He doesn't remember the exact words, but he says 'Mind your own business and stay out of there.' "

McGuirl's voice fell to almost a whisper, "David Smith gets into an argument. David Smith does something probably foolish, and it was borne out during this trial it was foolish, he punches him, he hits him, but that's the way it happened. Now what happens after he punches him? The defendant goes back and out comes the gun. Well, you're going to hear about self-defense and his Honor will tell you and you will realize as you listen to that and you can discuss it when you go back into the jury room, you cannot use deadly physical force, a gun, in response to physical force which is a punch. Some of you may have just known that on your own, just by thinking about it, but it is a law and you will hear it and listen to the law and follow it.

"The gun comes out and there is a statement, and we will deal with that, and the gun gets pointed—a peacemaker? Hit him in the leg or shoot at the building wall? What does the defendant do? Where would you shoot to kill? There are two places. One is right here, right in the heart. Where is the other place you shoot to kill? Right here, right in the head. How far off would you be? You heard from the doctor. A little higher up, it could have been in the brain. That's where you shoot to kill. The heart or the head. Where does the gun go? Does it go down to the leg? Does it go over to his arm? No, it comes up, goes to his head. How far away? A couple of feet. Points it at his head and then he shoots and he hits him and he hits him in the head. Now, in the direction he pointed that gun and he pulled the trigger, doesn't that tell you something? His head was where he was pointing. What is going to happen when he hits it? Well, don't let me tell you, He told you himself."

As McGuirl laid in his points about the crime, his voice grew more steely. He faced the jury squarely and chose his words carefully.

"Isn't that pretty clear what he was trying to do—'I want to kill you with a gun at the head?' Is David Smith in any danger with him, a completely unarmed man on your right? David is physically bigger, but he is no Wonder

Woman. He is not going to knock the bullets off with any bracelets or anything like that. What does he do when he gets hit? Do you remember where the wound was? The doctor says here on the left. What did David Smith tell you he was doing? He was going to take off. He was turning his head to take off. Started turning his head, and where did he get hit? Where was he starting to run? He was shooting a man who was about to run from you. Certainly not shooting to defend Cleo. You are certainly not shooting to defend yourself. You are certainly shooting him to kill him and he hits him and where does it strike, it goes right into the mouth. It is a nice head-on head shot. It would have done its job a little higher or a little bit lower. And then what happens next? David Smith runs off, runs to the hospital which is what he's started to do when he gets blasted in the head. And the defendant had his gun now and he just pointed it around and then he takes off. He's gone."

McGuirl touched on the other witnesses' testimony and then about the long search to find and arrest Fred Figures. He passed a hand across his forehead looking, for a moment, tired.

"And after all this information, several months later, Fred Figures is found, identified. No question Fred Figures is the shooter. No question, uncontradicted, that he possessed a loaded gun unlawfully. There is no question that he shot David Smith with a gun, caused physical injury to David Smith. There is no question that there is an unlawful use of a firearm, and there is no question when you think about where the gun was pointed and what was said at the same time the gun was pointed at the man who started to run, or his intent was to run.

"Well, a lot of people said you are in the community, a

lot of people want to hear what your verdict is going to be, and the community wants to know, 143rd Street wants to know what you're going to do. David Smith wants to know. Mark Smith wants to know. The defendant wants to know."

When McGuirl reached the end of his closing statement, he moved forward toward the jury box and stood completely still looking from one to the other.

"On behalf of the People of the State of New York, because the evidence demands it, I ask that you find the defendant guilty of all charges. Thank you."

The time had come for Judge Davis to charge the jury. In a somber tone, he made his instructions on their deliberations clear. Then he outlined the meaning of the charges against Fred Figures.

"You will decide the facts coolly, calmly and deliberately and without fear or favor or passion or prejudice or sympathy. As sole and exclusive judges of the facts, it is your sworn duty to decide the guilt or innocence of this defendant solely on the evidence admitted during the trial, and to pass judgement upon the evidence in the determination of all the issues."

As he went on, he defined the scope of the possible verdicts.

"Now, the first count of the indictment charges the defendant with the crime of attempted murder in the second degree as follows: The Grand Jury of the County of New York by this indictment accuses the defendant of the crime of attempt to commit the crime of murder in the second degree submitted as follows: The Defendant, in the County of New York, on or about August 17th, 1979, with intent to cause the death of David Smith, attempted to cause the death of David Smith by shooting him with a loaded pistol.

Since the crime charged is an attempt to commit murder as distinguished from the crime of murder itself, I shall first give you the legal definition of murder as it pertains to this case and then I will describe what an attempt to commit that crime is.

"Murder in the second degree, insofar as it is applicable to this case, is defined in our statute as follows: A person is guilty of murder in the second degree when, with intent to cause the death of another person, he causes the death of such person. A person is guilty of an attempt to commit a crime when, with the intent to commit a crime he engages in conduct which tends to effect the commission of such crime. Conduct means an act and its accompanying mental state."

"You will note that intent is the necessary element of the crime with which I have just described for you. Now, let me tell you what intent means. The law defines intent as follows: A person acts intentionally with respect to a result or to conduct described by a statute defining an offense when his conscious objective is to cause such result or to engage in such conduct. The intent with which a person commits an act or a crime is seldom, if ever, put into words by the person before the commission of the crime. Crimes are ordinarily secret and the person does not advertise or say beforehand what he intends to do. Intent is a secret, silent operation of a man's mind and the mental purpose to do a particular act or to achieve a definite result."

Finishing his instructions, the judge notified the jury that they would have to decide whether Fred Figures was guilty of possession of a weapon with intent to use it or mere possession. At this point the jury was led out of the courtroom.

They stayed out less than four hours. When they returned the clerk announced in his usual monotone, "Case on trial, the People against Fred Figures, is continued. Let the record indicate the defendant, the defendant's counsel and the Assistant District Attorney are present. Both sides stipulate that the twelve deliberating members of the jury are present?"

McGuirl nodded. "Yes."

Gonzalez said, "Yes."

The clerk turned to the jury. "Forelady of the jury, please rise. Has the jury reached a verdict?"

The juror spoke in a quiet, somber tone, "Yes." Her voice shook.

The clerk looked at her as if for the first time. "How do you find Count One of the indictment, the charge of attempted murder in the second degree?"

The juror rubbed her head thoughtfully and replied, "Guilty."

The clerk, his own voice softening, asked, "How do you find as to Count Three of the indictment, the charge of criminal possession of a weapon in the second degree as an armed felony? Guilty or not guilty?"

The juror, head down, said in a quiet but firm voice, "Guilty."

The clerk motioned to her. "You may be seated. Hearken to your verdict as it now stands recorded, you say through your forelady, that you find this defendant guilty of Count One of the indictment, the charge of attempted murder in the second degree, guilty, and Count Three of the indictment, the crime of criminal possession of a weapon in the second degree as an armed felony, guilty. Is that your verdict? Please answer collectively."

"Yes," the jury answered.

"So say you all." the clerk announced with dispatch.

As the sentencing hearing was convened, the clerk announced, "Case Number 3 on the sentence calendar. The People versus Fred Figures, Indictment Number 0829/80."

She indicated the defendant, "Fred Figures, is that your name? Is your attorney, Mr. Gonzalez, present?"

Figures rose and answered in a surly tone, "He's not my attorney!"

Judge Davis wasn't in the mood for comedy, "Let the record indicate that Mr. Gonzalez is sitting at the table. Mr. Gonzalez is the 18-B attorney appointed by the Appellate Division. Mr. Gonzalez was the attorney through the trial in this case and I recognize him as the attorney now."

The clerk continued, "Present for the People, Assistant District Attorney, Robert McGuirl."

Judge Davis, his patience sorely tried, went on, "Mr. Figures, I think you have a right to be your own attorney if you want to be, but, even if you are, I insist that Mr. Gonzalez help you.

"Now, this case is before me today first for motions. You will not be able to do that and Mr. Gonzalez will be able to make them.

"The case is set down for a persistent felony hearing which you know nothing, or very little, about, but which Mr. Gonzalez knows about. However, if you do want to act as your own attorney, I will give you an opportunity to do so with Mr. Gonzalez's help."

Later in the proceedings, Figures did make his statements known.

"Your Honor, I remember the first day like I came into your courtroom. You told me that you would see to it that I had a fair trial, you know, and, like, no way, impossible. Like what sentence is like, I understand this is your job, but, like for you to tell me that I had a fair trial under the circumstances in which this trial was tooken (sic.) place in this courtroom, there is no way possible that I could ever believe that I had a fair trial.

"You know, there was no proof beyond no reasonable doubt and there was no equal protection of the law. At any time a . . . one person can be found guilty for the same thing that his accuser is bringing forth." Figures kept going on and on. Despite Figures' lengthy argument, Judge Davis imposed a maximum, not a minimum, sentence.

"You are being sentenced by me as a predicate second violent felony offender. I think you were fortunate that it was decided that Mr. Gonzalez was able to point out that under the persistent felony statute that you didn't come in, at least the question arose and I resolved that in your favor.

"However, you are being sentenced by me as a second violent felony offender. You were found guilty by the jury on two counts. Count One of Attempted Murder in the Second Degree, which is a Class B Felony. You are being sentenced by me on that charge to a maximum term of twenty-five years and a minimum of twelve and a half years.

"You were found guilty of Count Three, which is Criminal Possession of a Weapon in the Second Degree, which is a Class C Violent Felony and, like the Attempted Murder, was a Class B Violent Felony. You are being sentenced by me on that count to a maximum term of fifteen years and a minimum of seven and a half.

"Both of these sentences to be run concurrently.

"However, all the sentences that I am imposing here now are to be consecutive to any time you are doing or that you now owe."

The Judge nodded to the clerk, who continued, "Fred Figures, you may appeal this conviction even though you have no funds. If you wish to appeal, you must file notice of this in this courtroom within thirty days. Let the record reflect that the Defendant has received a written notice of his right to appeal."

Judge Davis intervened, "Why don't you file a notice of appeal for him and he can take it from there."

Figures snapped back, "That's okay, your Honor. I'll file it myself."

And he did.

It was turned down.

The case, for all intents and purposes, was over.

14

Three Steps Forward, One Step Back

On the day the verdict was reached, Rita was asked by the judge not to attend the court session since her presence seemed to incite Fred Figures. She returned home from work that evening feeling tired and apprehensive. Sprawling across her living room couch, she tried to relax. Mc-Guirl was supposed to call. As the darkness closed in she kept picking up the telephone receiver from the table next to her just to check if the phone was working. It was.

An hour passed. Then two. Finally about 8:30 p.m. the phone rang. Rita grabbed it only to hear the voice of a Caucasian woman. "Mrs. Smith?" the woman said.

"Yes," Rita answered hesitantly, not knowing what to expect.

"You don't know me and it would be inappropriate of me to tell you my name because I'm one of the jurors. Have you heard the verdict?" The woman paused expectantly.

"No, I haven't." Rita said taking a deep breath.

"I want you to know that he was found guilty. I'm so happy about the verdict."

Rita let her breath out. "You're not the only one. We've been praying for it," she said gratefully.

"I want you to know something else," the woman went on. "Even though you weren't in that courtroom, everyone felt your presence—your spiritual presence. It was just like you were there. You have lovely sons and you've done a fine job with them."

"To hear that means a lot," Rita said earnestly. "It wasn't—."

The woman interrupted. "Rita, I'm involved with some nuns in a seminary upstate. I'm going to ask them to pray for you and your family." She paused. "I have to go but I wish you all the best of luck in the future, You're really an inspiration."

Before Rita could reply, the connection was broken.

Within an hour McGuirl called to relate the details of the verdict. Joyfully Rita gathered her children together and told them.

Unfortunately Fred Figures didn't leave Rita or her family's lives even though he was in prison. He was still very resentful that he was caught and felt that she had conspired to put him in jail.

Not long after he was convicted and incarcerated in Attica, Figures filed a lawsuit against Rita, her three sons and two of the police officers who were on the case. He sued them for ten thousand dollars.

When the Smith family received the summons, Rita was horrified. That meant that they had to get an attorney to answer his petition. Rita went down to the Federal Court to see if she could answer it herself. They said she had to get a lawyer. In her usual boisterous manner she protested. "Here I am with all these children and payments. A lawyer," she repeated, "I mean that's not in the budget."

Fred had written his own brief to the Court and Rita tried to call around to find someone who would help her do the same. Finally, she went to the law library and to the Conference of Black Lawyers on 119th Street. She told them that she wanted to see their books on constitutional law. The well-dressed clerk looked irritated. "Why don't you get an attorney?"

Rita answered, "Do you know how costly that is?"

He said, "Well you're middle class."

Rita replied, "What is middle class? After you go to college to get all these degrees, you've borrowed all this money, so you have all these loans. You owe the government your life. A middle class person in my position can't afford an attorney. Look, all I want to do is see your books and I'll write my own brief. I'll get the legal stationery and I'll prepare and submit it myself."

That same week she sent a letter to the court clerk and told him she couldn't afford lawsuits and asked how "Sonny" Figures could be in jail with the taxpayers' money paying for him to be there and suing people. Moreover, Rita wrote, "If Figures can submit his brief *pro se* (a phrase she picked up from the law books she was reading), I ought to be able to submit mine the same way."

Finally, they approved her right to do just that. Rita submitted her own brief, signed her name to it and hand carried it to Judge Sweet.

A few weeks later she went to court. The judge said, "Okay, it's fine. I'll take it into consideration and come up with a judgement."

And he did.

Judge Sweet declared the lawsuit basically invalid. As Rita said to her son and daughter commenting on Fred Figures, "He couldn't do anything to me insofar as saying that I had conspired with the police, because I was not a police officer. I was an individual citizen. In other words, I was not operating under as they say, 'the color of the law.' I was not a law enforcement person, so he could not sue me under the Civil Rights Act saying that I had done something wrong in violating his constitutional rights. He had gotten ahold of some law books and had decided he was going to be a jailhouse lawyer.

"And I don't think he expected to get such a long time in jail as twelve to twenty-five years. Because usually when it comes to black-on-black crime, they slap you on the wrist. So I was surprised myself."

A few weeks afterward her son David was able to get his teeth replaced. But everything was a battle.

First, Rita had to get an estimate on the work. And, as she said, "I couldn't get one dentist in Harlem to take the time to do an estimate on the work even though I was willing to pay for the examination. And I became very frustrated about that. So I said to hell with it. I looked in the classified section of the telephone book and saw the name of a dentist who did cosmetic dentistry on the stars. I decided that David would have the best. We would go to him."

At Jerry Lynn's plush office she said, "Whatever the fee for the x-rays, it's okay. I just need an estimate."

When Lynn asked what happened, Rita told him the story about Fred Figures shooting David and her struggle. He empathized. He said, "I'm going to fight with you. I'm going to help you. I know Charlie Rangel. I'll call him. It's only right that you should be compensated for this boy's teeth."

Doctor Lynn refused to even take the money for the x-rays. He gave Rita an estimate and went ahead and did the work before he got a dime. He said that he would do it anyway, even if he didn't get any money, because when he thought of Rita's struggle in Harlem and how she had to fight alone, he wanted to contribute something.

Afterward Rita and David had to go to the dental consultant that the state hired. At first, he didn't think the reconstruction was worth the amount of money Lynn had charged, but, finally, he did approve it. David got the work done and the dentist was paid.

As they went along, Rita learned, "It was like actually reaching out and making the next step before you walk it." If she couldn't get anyone in the community or local government who wanted to hear the story, she decided to just go to the top person. Rita found that sometimes she could get to the biggest person easier than to some of the small-time, small-minded people.

With David's mouth surgery successful, Rita's struggle to bring her family through the violence inflicted by Fred Figures was over, but her larger battle to rid her streets of drugs and rebuild them continued. With the momentum of the Smith family's victory over Fred Figures fresh in her neighbors' mind, Rita decided the next step was to organize a march on drugs.

She called everyone she knew and mailed out scores of circulars. Her plan was to march through 143rd Street, 142nd Street and all through Colonel Charles Young Park. In anticipation she began to make signs and bought some liberation flags. Some of the people she knew were very afraid, but she scheduled the march anyway for Saturday morning.

A few days before the scheduled march, Rita informed the police and was able to get a bullhorn from the precinct. Some of the police even offered to walk in the march. Then the lieutenant assigned some detectives, someone from Community Relations, and the inspector offered a police officer to stop traffic along the way.

But Saturday morning, when Rita was waiting for everyone to come, she called one neighbor and said, "Are you ready?"

He sounded very hesitant and said, "We-e-ll, sort of. I just had breakfast." But from the sound of it, Rita thought the breakfast had not done much to pick him up and maybe had done more to slow him down.

And then when she called Mrs. Russell, a feisty little woman from South Carolina Rita knew as a kid, and Mrs. Russell was hesitant. Rita decided that everybody had to have a little taste of something to give them the spark they needed to step out. So she said to Mrs. Russell, "Are you coming over?"

Mrs. Russell replied, "When you go across the street, then I'll come over."

"Okay," Rita answered, "Watch for me."

Rita, head high, followed by her children, strode downstairs and collected her first two marchers. Next, some of the elderly residents came out, residents with stories a lot like Mrs. Russell's.

Mrs. Russell was a milliner and had worked in the garment district. She had lived an active life and retired to her little apartment, ready to settle down and be rewarded. But all of a sudden, she had to get out and deal with this huge drug problem she had never expected.

There were others—elderly men and women who had enough heart to come out and look more closely at what had happened on their street and say, "Now let me see what I can do about this."

Others started gathering. People from across the city. People like Florence Rice, the famous consumer activist from Harlem who brought marchers from her area. And various people had heart enough to join in. Even Rita's ex-husband showed up. And then they started marching. Rita led the chant. "Down with drugs. Drugs must go!"

Neighbors looked out their windows. Some came down to join in. Mothers with baby carriages. Old people on canes.

At one point the line mysteriously dwindled and Rita didn't see some of those who had been there. She called out, "What happened to everybody?"

One of the marchers called back, "They went to put in the first number. They'll be back."

"Life goes on," Rita shouted back, remembering her mother's fascination with the numbers. Raucous laughter broke up the seriousness for a few minutes.

After that every once in a while Rita heard someone whisper, "What's the first number?"

And another person would answer, "Okay, now you go get the money." She laughed as one and then another marcher broke away for a while to collect.

Rita couldn't help thinking that there was nothing like the people of Harlem. They were so delightful and so real.

Along the way more people joined the march. They would say, "I'm sick of this. Look at those marchers. Let's get in line with them."

As they went along, the marchers stopped in front of all the places where they felt dealers were selling drugs—the abandoned buildings, the stores. Those inside stared while the marchers shouted. "Down with drugs. Down with drugs!"

The marchers began to set the chant to a little tune and made it rhyme. That really gave the people spirit and heart. Even though the marchers may have been fearful, they kept marching and singing. They made a stand. They regained their sense of being real human beings, the sense of being true to themselves.

At the end of the march, Rita made a short speech.

"Now listen. Life is not worth living if we have to live half a life, if we have to be afraid to come out of our apartments. Walk in our neighborhood. What purpose is it? It's very difficult for people like us to fight a whole community. You have to have the whole community with you." She paused. "And you are the community. Not them. Apart, they will defeat us but together, we can take back our streets."

15

Honey and Lye

---

*B*ecause of the police raids and the people's march, the residents of 143rd Street had begun to see results, the kind of results one doesn't usually see in Harlem where mostly people are apathetic, where mostly you call the police and they seldom show up. But suddenly the police were showing up. Rita and her neighbors had begun to communicate with them and they were seeing some action.

Of course, as soon as the police would pick up the dealers, they'd be back on the street. Rita asked herself, 'What do we do about that?' Finally, she spoke to some neighbors.

"Why don't some of you go down to court when these guys are taken there?"

Rita and her neighbors started doing just that—being participants in the court, showing up from 143rd Street with a sign, "DRUGS MUST GO." The court official would ask that they put their sign down, but the judge had already seen it. He knew he was going to have to start dealing with the people. When the defendants were called, the entire group would stand up.

The prosecutor would then say, "Those are the residents of 143rd Street, your Honor." And then he would say, "Please sit down ladies and gentlemen." When it all was over, Rita would lead the group out of the courtroom together. Sometimes there were as many as a dozen 143rd Street residents attending the trials.

Always there were Mrs. Russell, Mr. Larch, Tilmon Gibbs and Maria Alvaranga. Everybody was learning, basically, the ropes of the system and it was stimulating their minds. Each was getting ideas about the things that a person could do. Rita began giving them research projects and giving them the names of contacts so they would know where to go to get things done.

Tilmon Gibbs was interested in co-oping his building. To do that meant he had to touch base with Housing Preservation and Development, one of the community agencies, the Community Service Society, etc., Rita showed him how.

Mrs. Russell wanted her landlord to put a locked door on the building and make other improvements. With Rita's help, Mrs. Russell got up a petition. Everybody was getting ideas about how they could better their immediate environment. They made plans to get representatives for each building and to monitor the activities.

It wasn't a matter of being ignorant of the system; they just didn't believe in the system. So they didn't bother with it. Like so many people in Harlem, they didn't believe that anything was ever going to change because the system was oppressive and designed to continue to be oppressive.

They hadn't ever seen anything change for them. It was the same story all the time. Harlem had the highest rate of unemployment; the people were very aware of poor health care; they paid the highest money for food. They saw what was going on and saw that no one was changing anything, and so felt what could they do?

Most people had a fear of dealing with the system. They could deal with Rita, but to go downtown in that cold, antiseptic environment was very hard and intimidating. A lot of people just gave up. But once they started attending meetings with Rita, they felt her energy and commitment and began to get their spunk up.

One of the first to participate was her co-marcher Mrs. Russell. She was, at this time, sixty-eight years of age and had lived in Harlem for more than thirty years.

Mrs. Russell was a tiny woman, about four-feet-nine, but she was feisty—the kind of lady who, once she became aroused, would fight for her rights. Having come from South Carolina, she explained that her life wasn't easy before coming up north, that she had struggled hard in her early years, but that she admired two equally spunky women of her generation: Eleanor Roosevelt and Mary McLeod Bethune, the black woman who had advised Franklin Delano Roosevelt.

One night Rita and her neighbors, including Mrs. Russell, held a 143rd Street block association meeting at Minisink Townhouse, a community center on Lenox Avenue. As Rita spoke, she described what the police's role should now be in continuing their drug fight. She described their own street's improvement in fighting drugs but commented that behind and in front and to each side were blocks where drug dealing was rampant. She went on to detail the part they would all have to play to clean up those surrounding blocks. As she reached the climax of her speech she became more and more impassioned.

"Do you remember how Rosa Parks down there in Montgomery, Alabama in 1953, said she wasn't going to go to the back of the bus?" Rita asked. "She didn't take it, did she? That's what we here on 143rd need to do now."

The people in the audience agreed. "That's right," they shouted as they began to move around in their seats and nod to each other.

Rita could see that some of them were getting really excited. There was more than anger in the room, there was an energy waiting to be channeled into action. Before she could restrain herself, she shouted, "get them to clean up the rest of our neighborhood!" She stamped her foot and clapped her hands for emphasis.

Around her, people stamped and yelled back, "That's right. That's right!" And at that, most of the roomful of young mothers, senior citizens, and adolescents jumped up, marching in place.

Rita was caught off guard. They really wanted to march again. Right then. She tried to quiet them down so that she could impart some semblance of an agenda. "Now listen," she said, "when we go into the precinct, everybody's going to be cool and calm. I'll be the spokesman."

With that, the group flooded out of the townhouse and into the Harlem night. As they marched to the precinct, they sang civil rights songs and laughed about how impetuous they were. Some of the folks were grandmothers and grandfathers and here they were acting on impulse like kids on a Friday night dare.

On the way, Mr. Bell caught up with Rita near the front of the line. He declared, "Rita, I feel so GOOD! Now I know what it was like for Martin Luther King and all of those people when they marched. Rita, you're helping me to be a man."

And that meant so much to him. He must have felt degraded being so afraid of drug dealers in his apartment that he had to ask Rita and her sons to walk him home. He was probably ashamed of himself for not being able to stand up. Men are supposed to be strong and stand up, but on this block, mostly women were involved.

But that night, he was as delighted as a little boy just finding out something new about himself. He said, "You don't know how my blood is just flowing! Now when are we going to march again?"

The precinct on 135th Street was a good ten-block walk, long enough that the group used up much of their charged adrenaline, but far enough that they had time to decide that they were going to demand real action from the police. It was almost 10 p.m. by the time they arrived.

As they filed up the steps, Rita whispered to the activists that she would approach the night desk sergeant and make a statement on behalf of them all. Then they would request that the police take all the complaints. Everyone was to make an individual complaint. That way, the commander and the rest of the precinct would be forced to deal with the future prospect of a group of crazy community people who might sometime again descend upon their police station and bring things to a standstill with a ton of paperwork.

The night sergeant was a woman. When seventy-five demonstrators walk into a place, even on their best behavior, there's bound to be a commotion. There was. People came in talking and laughing and shushing each other. The sergeant looked up in both surprise and exasperation. "Please. Can we have some order in here?" she asked.

And that was all the cue that Rita needed. She stepped right up to the sergeant and, in her most demur tone, said, "Yes, Ma'am. We believe in law and order too, and we're here to help you achieve it, not only on our block, but in our neighborhood and we have come complaints that the police haven't heard yet."

"All these people?" the sergeant asked in shock.

"Yes, you have to talk to them all tonight."

"Well, I'm the only one here."

"Well, I'm sorry about that," Rita lied.

Everyone started telling the sergeant their names and making their individual complaints. They were all nice and polite and time-consuming. They stayed at the precinct until nearly one a.m., until the sergeant had processed the last anecdote and detail about crime on the block given by the last person in the entourage.

Rita imagined that the sergeant had a major case of writer's cramp that night. But she also knew that the experience with the group would not be dismissed lightly by the commanding officer.

At the same time, Rita and her neighbors were letting the police know that the people of 143rd Street were going to support their actions and wanted more of their presence.

Rita also decided to seek support from the local

churches. One of the parishioners of St. Charles Borromeo Roman Catholic Church on West 142nd felt that his pastor, Monsignor Emerson Moore, should get involved. Some of his parishioners were scared to even go to church.

Two nights later, when the marchers reconvened, they went straight to his church. Monsignor Moore had what looked like a swarm of police officers already there. Mrs. Russell looked at them and asked mischievously, "What are you all here for? To arrest us or what?"

Finally, the serious part of the meeting got under way. Rita thanked the police for their good work on 143rd Street, but said it wasn't enough. Every time the children went to school or when anyone shopped around the corner or on the next block the drug traffic confronted them.

The police representative spoke up and told the group why they couldn't block off the streets, and why they couldn't randomly arrest suspicious persons. They talked about the restrictions that they were under in solving the drug problems on the block. They talked about the routines they had to observe before they could arrest drug possession suspects. Even as Rita and her neighbors sat there, drug dealers were calling out the names of their products right across the street from Monsignor Moore's church.

Finally, after listening to the bureaucratic line, Mrs. Russell had had enough. "We can't deal with all of this bureaucracy," she told them. "You know they're breaking the law; we know they're breaking the law, and we want the dealers permanently removed from 143rd Street. Not just raids, after which they're right back on our street. So far, the only things that you all have told us about is what you CAN'T do. Well, I'm gonna tell you what I'm GONNA do."

They replied, "Okay, Mrs. Russell, what are you going to do?"

"Now, I'm going to get me a bowl and in that bowl I'm going to mix me some lye and some honey. And I'm gonna to throw me a batch of lye-and-honey on the first drug dealer I catch in my hallway. Do you understand?"

A few persons registered amazement that this elderly widow could even suggest using violence, while others sent up snickers. "Why you gotta mix it with honey?' someone managed to ask her.

"Because it sticks, damn it," she answered in a high-pitched voice. "It sticks."

Not long afterward Mrs. Russell had a chance to show that her drug fighting technique was more than amusing. It was potent.

Accosted in her apartment house by one of the dealers, a wiry, sports coat clad teenager who had snuck in unde-tected, Mrs. Russell grabbed him by the collar with one hand. With the other, she took from her shopping bag a cellophone wrapped bowl filled with her remedy.

"Do you know what this is?" she yelled at her assailant.

"What is it old lady? Pudding?" the boy said smugly.

"You wish," Mrs. Russell said firmly. "It's honey and lye."

He wrenched away from her, shielding his eyes.

"And if I ever catch you near here again," Mrs. Russell said determinedly, "I'm going to throw it first and talk after-ward. Do you understand?" Holding his head in his hands, the dealer quickly made for the stairway. "And remember, don't come back," she yelled after him.

It was an incident that people smiled at and spoke of for weeks. Mrs. Russell showed them that old people weren't helpless.

Mr. Lavelle, another one of Rita's neighbors, decided on a way he could contribute to the cause. "I'm going to line up some flowerpots and some bricks on my windowsill," he said. "If I catch one of them dope-selling or dope-buying so-and so's under my window . . . BOOM! I'm going to bomb 'em!"

Pretty soon, everybody was using their ledges like castle keeps. Instead of boiling vats of hot oil, they heated pots of hot water to pour down on the milling packs. Rita kept her hose upstairs and hung it out the window to spray hot water on the pushers.

Every now and then some unsuspecting touter would yelp in pain and then curse and the neighbors would know that another member of the window resistance had stung his or her target. Even when they'd miss, the sight of a nearby flying flowerpot landing on the sidewalk or the vibrating impact of a three-pound brick would make the unwelcome visitors move on. The sidewalks that had been so easy for the dealers and touters to take over were becoming increasingly treacherous.

From then on, whenever Rita personally confronted any of the drug dealers, one or more of her neighbors would step out of their buildings where the pushers could see them and support her.

In addition, the Quality of Life Unit, the police group which had made the first dent in drug operations on the street with its raids, offered further help. One day Pranzo suggested, "We'll give you a two week all clear." He told Rita to warn all the other residents of the block they were not to loiter, to just go in and out. Rita explained to her neighbors what would be happening.

During that two week period, due to a heavy police visability on the block, there was peace on 143rd Street. No fire engines, no fires in the abandoned buildings, and there was a sense of calm, a level of homeostasis. Suddenly the residents could sleep like human beings. They knew the other side of the coin—what it had been like and, now, what it could be like. And they liked what it could be like.

As a result of that two week period, they became even more ready to stand up. "I can't have my sleep disturbed. I can't be running out." That's what Miss Ann and Timon Gibbs said.

And once people on the block saw their efforts further rewarded, everybody started getting into it.

Rita and her neighbors became hawk-like in noticing descriptions of people who tried to market narcotics on their block. When they passed these strangers on the sidewalks making illegal transactions, they'd hold their eyes just a little longer on the dealers' faces. Or they would peer down from windows. One of the best block watchers, Mary Bell, even kept binoculars next to her window so she could peep out and spot where those guys hid drugs. Rita's neighbors had now become first-class, urban reconnaissance agents. They jotted down whatever didn't look right and then contacted the police.

At about the same time, the police started vertical patrols, going up into high-rises and abandoned buildings where they routed addicts. Sometimes they would knock a door down and inside would be junkies lying around on the floor, nodding and drooling. Sometimes the police found that they had injected their hypodermics of heroin into the only fresh spots on their bodies where they hadn't yet built up scar tissue—their testicles, in their armpits or under their tongues.

Although the narcotics team was designed to raid locations all over the precinct, Pete Pranzo focused on 143rd Street. During the next month, he again made large raids with back-up from other precinct police.

In the raids, they took dozens of drug suspects at a location. Soon it dwindled down to five or ten, but it was still a constant battle every day for possession of the area.

The police made most of their sweeps on 143rd Street based on the residents' observations. Most of that time, Mrs. Russell was on the case like a block observer. She saw everything that was going on and reported incidents to Rita. She gave Rita licence plate numbers and personal descriptions, who was carrying the drugs, who was holding the money, who the steerers were, who the lookouts were and the like. She and the people of the community became Rita's eyes and ears. Rita, in turn, did all of the contacting and the negotiating with the system, including making the telephone calls.

There was still a barrier between the police and the people in the community. They wondered, "Well, can we trust a police force whose administration is all white?"

But Rita felt they had no choice. "Let's work with the police. Let's work with Peter." She knew their efforts on 143rd Street would work if they could just follow the leader. They didn't have any infighting about who was going to lead. At first they all assumed that whatever decisions needed to be made in the organization, Rita would make them, and they would take the responsibility delegated to them. But Rita knew that if the movement was to really succeed, each of the group had to be able to reach out and handle the inevitable crises themselves. She began to coach them on how to contact the police or whoever was needed.

Gradually Miss Ann would call Pranzo herself. Then Virginia began to call. Even Mr. Bell, who had discovered his courage, was able to call the police to report drug dealers in his hallway. "Come and get these guys," he would say. Soon, when Bell would find pushers in his hallway, instead of shrinking by to walk past them, he'd demand, "Now YOU step aside! You don't live here. You get out of here."

Rita also talked to Pranzo. She knew if the police didn't respond promptly, the people would become discouraged. The contact would stop.

When he got the calls, Pranzo made every effort to follow through. He'd send a big paddy wagon and, from the other end of the block, he'd come in the car where dealers didn't expect him because 143rd Street is a one-way street.

The police would jump out of the cars and the wagon, quickly catch the dealers and users, line them all up against the wall, frisk them, and make the suspects take their shoes and socks off in order to check for drugs. Pranzo made sure he was in the thick of things. At first people hadn't trusted him, but later, as his efforts succeeded, they would cheer him on.

By this time, the police department's public relations office had notified the press that the drug trade was under attack on 143rd Street, a place the *Village Voice* had called a "major drug retail outlet."

They let newspaper columnist, Earl Caldwell, know about the fight the residents were waging to reclaim the block. Caldwell was a columnist with *The Daily News*. He wrote about events that affected the city's and nation's black community.

Caldwell came up and saw for himself what the story on 143rd Street was. He found it compelling and committed to letting his readers know about it. His editorials brought Rita and her group plenty of publicity. One of Caldwell's readers was Mayor Ed Koch, who called Rita to say "I'm with you."

At that point Rita began to feel that the better day of which she had once dreamed was about to happen. Suddenly another problem surfaced.

At the time Rita was working for Bayview Correctional Facility, but the executive director at Bayview wasn't too happy with all the articles in the paper about Rita or her block. He called Rita and told her to "cool it."

Rita replied, "How are you going to tell me to cool it? That's where I live. That has nothing to do with my job."

Shortly thereafter, she went to work one day and wasn't allowed to go into the prison. The sergeant said, "Oh, Mrs. Smith. I am so sorry, but I have been told by South Forty that you are no longer coordinator of the program."

Rita had been terminated without her knowledge. When she went to her office, they wouldn't let her in. She waited outside. When the sergeant came out, she asked him if she could go get her things since she hadn't even been given a one-day notice.

"I'm sorry," he said shaking his head. "No unauthorized visits."

The guards brought Rita's personal effects to her in a box and wordlessly Rita took it, put the box in the trunk of her car and, feeling tears trickle down her cheeks, drove away.

Afterwards she called the precinct and spoke to Pete Pranzo. She said, "You know, Inspector, I have had it."

"What happened, Rita?" he asked.

Rita told him about being fired. "It seems that life is really not worth anything here. You have to fight for the basic right to live and, I mean, it's ridiculous that you can't make too much noise about things like drugs out on the streets. It's awful to even live like this."

Pranzo was sympathetic but firm, "Rita, you knew it wasn't going to be easy. Cheer up now."

Tearfully, but resolutely, Rita agreed.

16

Planting Roses in Cement

---

*R*ita was now without an income because of her activism and the publicity which was helping her to drive drug dealers from 143rd Street. When she tried to collect her severance pay, prison officials told her the check had been sent by certified mail. For almost six weeks nothing arrived. But Rita's friends helped her survive. Some, at the Catholic Worker, sent her a food allowance until she could get unemployment.

Applying for unemployment was an unwanted, unwarranted lesson in despair. Rita had fought so hard and so long to be independent, to take care of herself and her children. And here she was, a college graduate, back taking a handout again. She hated it, but the money kept her family together, gave her a chance to decide how to cope and a chance to work on her big project, getting the block rebuilt.

It was, she decided later, a blessing in disguise. Looking for the right job, she stayed on unemployment until about May of that year. At that point, her marriage had also come to an end. She was alone again, with seven children to support. Then Rita realized she had to pay the kids' tuitions come September. She could not be particular. Swallowing her pride she went to the unemployment office to ask for any available employment in social work or in another field. The caseworker said, "What about a job at Harlem Hospital?"

Rita was about to object to the location when she realized that she didn't want to work at any of the nonprofit agencies, because it was too easy to lose a job as she had hers. If a politician called and he didn't like you, you were out. She didn't plan to sit back and become meek about drugs, so chances were, she was going to lock horns with some politician again. The only way she could get around this was to get a city job. If she got a city job, she thought, it would be hell to get rid of her. She would have to be highly incompetent and then they'd have to deal with the social work board. It wasn't easy to get rid of someone when the person was locked into one of those civil service jobs. Without further vacillation, she decided to seek the job at Harlem Hospital.

The hours were from 7 a.m. to 3 p.m. which meant she would still be home early enough to work on the block project. She could still keep the ball rolling.

She applied, went on the interview and got the job.

Ironically, Rita learned later that the number one reason she got the position was that it involved working in a very difficult area with drug-addicted patients. When Rita first heard the details she didn't think that she could take it. She said, "Lord, you would have thought I'd had enough of these drugs. Now I'm going to work with them on a fulltime basis, too." But then she realized that she needed to understand the psyche of drug-addicted people, to find out why people get involved in drugs. Again she plunged in.

On the first day she found, much to her further disillusionment, that the job locale was an outpost, not even in Harlem Hospital, but at 118th street, a rough neighborhood between 8th and St. Nicholas. It was as bad, if not worse, than 143rd Street before her campaign to clean it up.

Arriving in a stylish gray suit, the patients stared at her, laughed and whispered. One of the patients, a thin, ebony-skinned man whose lined face made him look sixty instead of the thirty he was, asked her, "What are you doing here? Whatchoo know about drug addicts? You don't know nothing about being addicted. Whatchoo know?"

With her usual aplomb Rita answered, "Well, honey, you sure don't have to step in shit to know it stinks." That sort of chilled her critics out.

Afterward, as Rita began to work among the addicts, to find them resources and show them humanity, they responded to her honesty and dedication. They wanted people to like them and most people didn't because of their drug problems. As she learned the ropes, Rita found that the addicts were the most difficult population to advocate for as far as getting services because of the nature of their condition. As she said, "If you're talking about finding them apartments, nobody wants them. If you're talking about getting them treatment, they're put on waiting lists." Meeting drug addicts on a one-to-one basis confounded some of her myths. Because most of those with whom Rita came in contact were at the beginning of their addictive careers, many of them still worked and she found that most of their families never even knew they were addicted.

In taking their psychological histories, she also found some striking similarities. Most had gotten caught up in drug addiction very early in life, during the period of adolescence and puberty. And, once they made that one mistake, it was made for a lifetime. Their emotional development was stunted. In essence, Rita ended up dealing with adult children. They had never progressed beyond adolescence because of their drug problems and focusing on getting drugs. Other nurturing experiences just didn't take place.

Moreover, most of them developed multiple addictions. Alcohol, pills, other kinds of drugs and all kinds of related diseases, in addition to their original drug of choice, surfaced later. They would look relatively well when she first met them but, as time went on, those who did not commit to treatment destroyed their bodies and eventually their minds.

Bob, an addict who she befriended, would come to Rita's office whenever he came to the clinic. He was a handsome young man but, as time went on, confessed to taking a variety of drugs. As they talked out his problems, Rita felt pangs of grief. This could have been one of her children. She was determined to help him.

"Now this is off the record," she told him after several months. "I'm not talking about social work. I'm talking about what's real and what's human. I think that you maybe have to read the Book. Get some strength from the Bible. Get some faith because that's what has always helped me."

One of the Korean doctors, Dr. Chew, who was a born-again Christian, began a Bible class. Rita told Bob about it. For a while, the young man seemed better. But one day when he came to see Rita his words were slurred, his face blotched and swollen. Rita knew immediately he was on something again. When he left, she felt completely discouraged.

For a long time she didn't see him. Several years passed. When they met again, Bob had gotten married and had become a minister. He told her that he began to pray a short time after their discouraging meeting. Then he became involved in a Bible class, and it helped him to get his act together.

Rita saw few such transformations, but some of the addicts she worked with successfully took Methadone therapy and she was able to get them apartments and change the quality of their lives for the better. Even these small advances seemed heartening.

In addition, she was able to get the hospital officials to initiate different systems regarding case conferences and established a lot of new policies that didn't exist before she came.

Through one, she developed a workshop called "Short Term Options for Personal Transition." It dealt with the dynamics that make people what they are. In the sessions, she tried to help the addicts focus on themselves and to do things to make them look and feel better. One of the things she did was have the addicts practice walking with dignity so that they could show pride in themselves. Some of those simple techniques helped raise their levels of self-esteem.

Rita's workshops ran for six week periods. After each one terminated, Rita held a ceremony and presented the participants with certificates stating that they had successfully completed the course. Rita knew a lot of these people had never gotten anything before; they never graduated from high school and never received a diploma with their names on it that said they had done something and done it well. The closing ceremony was a good experience for them. It gave them a feeling of closure, of completion.

At the same time that Rita was learning about the psyche of drug addicts and how to rehabilitate them, her block movement to drive the drugs out of her neighborhood was gaining momentum. Rita and the people of 143rd Street had begun reaching out to city officials and connecting.

As head of the housing preservation committee, Rita had set out to investigate the ownership of all those abandoned buildings on her block. In each state there is a housing department that usually has records of all the real property in that particular city or township. There you can find out who owns the property. In 143rd Street's case, the owner of record was the City of New York. As Rita continued to research into which funds were available for fixing up city-owned properties that were partly occupied as well as those that were totally vacant, she and her group made contact with the head of the unit that would handle that specific area of housing development.

A heavy-set, overworked bureaucrat, he gruffly insisted, "There's just no new money for redevelopment."

Hearing that, Rita just pressed on. She came up with
another idea. "Then maybe there's some existing money
that can be used," she countered.

And, of course, there were a variety of programs that
the city operated under which the tenants could co-op their
buildings or renovate them. Indeed, there was a limited
amount of Section 8 money that was to go toward a Harlem
project. Again it was a matter of writing to the right people
to obtain it.

Rita worked tirelessly. She contacted everybody in the
City, in every department. She made appointments and
went to see them, taking some of the people from the community along. Together, they told the officials what they
wanted to do.

Then Rita drew up a plan and talked about the block.
"Who came first? Was it the abandoned buildings or was it
the drug dealers?" she asked.

Of course, Rita talked about the abandonment, which
meant they had an opening, a place for the dealers to come,
because there wasn't anyone in the area except women who
were heading households on their own, older people and
others who simply did not have the ability to move because
of various personal restrictions.

After much discussion it was agreed that Rita and her
group could have the Section 8 money. A developer was
also found to work with the group.

It was an interesting match. Developers and community groups seldom have a good relationship. And, as Rita
said, "We just had a shotgun wedding. We were just working
on the birth of this baby, that's 143rd Street again."

The developer and his staff had a lot of differences with Rita in regard to how she saw the community and how they should plan the housing. Despite advice to "cool it," advice she had heard before, she gave them a lot of input.

"Women have to maintain the household and take care of the children so there are certain things within the structure of our domain that have to be—the kitchen, enough closet space etc. You're not going to cut up these apartments," she said firmly, "because we need room, we need air, we need lights and a little area for a garden. At times the builders were sick of me. Construction is a very male-oriented field. The architects, the planners, the developer, they were all men, but they had to put up with Miss Rita."

As the plans became more concrete, all of Rita's group became more active. They loved to get dressed up and go down and see the bureaucrats. Some like Mrs. Russell were confrontational almost from the beginning. Others like Mrs. Alvaranga didn't get involved on that level. She might observe something and she might see, but she would very quietly point it out to Rita

On the other hand, Mrs. Russell was wonderful because she'd "tell it like it is." Rita would talk with the officials very eloquently and, when it got out of hand, she would just tap Mrs. Russell on the knee.

Mrs. Russell would get up and say, "Now let me just tell you one damn thing." Then she would make her point very effectively.

Gradually even Mrs. Alvaranga began to speak up. In the visits back and forth to the city, the officials' stories would change. First, they would tell one story, then another. Mrs. Alvaranga would listen very intently and be very apologetic. Then one day she popped up, "I thought you said that you were going to do so-and-so." Angrily, she hammered her fist on the table top.

Rita looked up shocked. She couldn't imagine Mrs. Alvaranga acting in that manner.

Mrs. Alvaranga continued. "Just hold it. Now let me tell you one damn thing. Now you know I've been coming down here for months and you've been screwing me with a wooden cock. And it's hurting, man."

Rita thought she had never heard anything so funny. Mrs. Alvaranga of all people. Rita was convulsed with laughter.

Over the next months, members of the preservation group drew together and proceeded to take care of business. They had learned the mechanism of teamwork.

Rita tried to teach them what to look out for. If one and one didn't add up to two when they visited these agencies, then something was wrong. At first, she would just hold up her hand and say "Listen." It was the key word.

The group would listen more closely to the architects and the developers and say, "No, no, no. That doesn't sound right." Then the group would take the developers to task so they couldn't put one over on them.

In the meantime, as the group progressed, they began to reach high priority people. After the mayor came to the group's gathering, people all over New York started to take more notice.

Mayor Koch announced, "Housing had to be built in stages. But we gave preference to Dr. Smith's block because of her courage against the drug pushers even when no new housing was being built.

"Our Housing and Preservation Department gave preference to her block because of those people's courage in not running away, but instead, driving the drug pushers off the block. You could call it political if you call it political to reward civic courage. You can't redeem a neighborhood where people have no leadership and where they aren't willing to help. That neighborhood had leadership and the people are willing to fight to redeem where they lived."

The drug dealers heard, and the people on surrounding streets heard. Everyone began to have more respect for the group who was rebuilding 143rd Street because now people on a high level were listening. And, of course, that inspired more commitment among the members of the preservation group. And others who now wanted to join. After that, Rita's main job was to maintain the momentum.

Finally, Rita and the preservation group got their first taste of real success. It was a small bit of nourishment, but it was very sweet. The city came in and sealed up thirty-four abandoned buildings.

17

The Ruin Restored—
Building a
Neighborhood Again

Sealing up the abandoned buildings was the first step in permanently ridding West 143rd Street of addicts and dealers. But, unless these easily accessible breeding grounds for heroin could be closed for good and then renovated, Rita knew that other kinds of dope users (by this time marijuana, angel dust and even cocaine were being sold) and sellers would appear. Without a plan to rehabilitate these buildings the efforts of Rita and her neighbors would be worthless. They would only clear away one group of undesirables to make room for another.

Rita had a plan. She believed it was a good one, but

while she was trying to rally support for it, there were several steps forward and a few steps back.

There were many abandoned buildings on the street. It was a constant battle to keep the area clear. Someone would go into an abandoned building and sleep there and start with the drugs again. Then the preservation group would have the building sealed up. After that junkies would sometimes break in and they had to be resealed again.

At one point, Rita got so tired of hearing people's complaints that she felt she knew the police precinct's number better than she knew her own phone number.

Then, one snowy day in 1981, a weary and shivering Rita drove home from Harlem Hospital where she had attended a long staff meeting. Suddenly, she spotted a huge yellow bulldozer gobbling up chunks of brown earth and grey cement in the middle of her block.

Quickly parking her car Rita jumped out and ran across the street. She yelled joyfully, "Glory to God in the highest. Finally. Finally. Finally the ruin is going to be restored."

She began to stride towards the bulldozer, but, as Rita approached the truck, she stopped short, standing absolutely still for a few moments, remembering something she had heard long before about bulldozers coming into Harlem driven by the people who once owned the land. As she moved forward and reached out to touch the giant machine, Rita wondered what was going to happen to Harlem, to its people. Because all this was going to be very painful for them, especially the elderly, who from then on would be part of and have to deal with a world they didn't even really know about. This would be a hard struggle. To adjust to changes they hadn't made and didn't want while still trying to hold onto those things that were vital in their lives. Their furniture, their little apartments and the people they knew once upon a time.

But Rita also knew that what was so wonderful was that these people had begun to believe in themselves. She saw hope, in the fact that they wanted to do something about the problems which existed. The greatest thing was that people had become aware and enlightened and empowered. And it had happened to them and to her.

Everybody had assumed some responsibility in this project. They'd put everything in the pot to come up with some sort of resolution. And when Rita saw everyone begin to operate on their own, stand up and become vocal, she saw the fear leaving them. Maybe believing that together they could make a change, was the thing that really fed and rejuvenated her; the fact that she was able to say, "See?", and they saw.

They were willing to stick with it. The beginning nucleus of her preservation group was a very small number, but they had believed in her. They had faith that Rita was educated, that she was knowledgable.

Now, as she stood there in the fading sunlight looking at the bulldozer, she resolved again that if they would continue to have faith in her, she would remain committed to them. In truth, she believed God was helping her to do this and would see her through. And she went on blind faith that the changes which were taking place were in accordance with His Plan, that the things which were now beginning to happen would be positive ones.

And for the most part, they were.

By 1982, there wasn't any drug market on 143rd Street. There might have been a couple of individuals occasionally trying to come in and sell drugs where they could, but the neighborhood hawks would get them out by calling the police to come and get the junkies in order to maintain the drug-free status of the block. The Quality of Life police team was still active.

There was a lot of publicity. Rita was doing all kinds of documentaries for television talking about the area. Film crews were coming in with cameras. Bill Boggs did a documentary on the block. Channel 2's Fred Noriega and Carol Martin and Poncietta Pierce from Channel 4 all came to 143rd Street. There was a lot of talk about the area and, as a result, everyone in the city began looking more closely at 143rd Street and watching what would happen.

The highlight of Rita's efforts came a few months later when she successfully negotiated for eleven million dollars to rehabilitate the first building on 143rd Street, another on 144th Street and some of the surrounding area. The eleven million dollars was the last of the city's federal Section 8 housing money for rehabilitating run-down buildings.

However, Rita soon learned that successfully negotiating, acquiring and then utilizing state funds are separate transactions. Another year passed as Rita and her preservation group endured a rocky relationship with architects and developers as they tried to finalize plans for what she thought had already been agreed to as to the space and services which would exist.

During that same year Rita received the *Wonder Woman Award* given to outstanding women of the community. At the ceremony, the reasons why she had been given the award were described. "In every part of this country, there are women who, at some point in their lives, have the courage to look at themselves in the bright light of honesty.

What they see is always wonderful, and always terrifying. Wonderful because their abilities are always greater than they could possibly have realized. Terrifying because they are, at first, afraid to use them." It was one of several awards Rita received during that period as well as having her story told on the television show "This Is Your Life."

From 1982 to 1984 the first two buildings were being renovated. At the ground-breaking, Rita invited all of the police who had been part of her Quality of Life team to participate.

As she explained at the ceremony, "What begins to happen when people deal with each other on an ongoing basis is they begin to view each other differently. Racism and all these other things may exist on both sides, but once you develop a relationship, you begin to work together and things begin to happen for the good. You begin to see people in a new light. You begin to see people as people.

"The police began to know us as people from the community. Mrs. Alvaranga who makes those nice Jamacian cakes. Mrs. Russell's little laugh. And they begin to like you as a person and the fact that you're spunky. I mean, this is the police and the community. We also came to like them better. What was changing was attitudes. After a while as the police would pass in the police cars, everybody would wave at them and say "How ya doing?" There was a warm relationship developing. We are here today to celebrate, in part, what has happened because of that relationship. Because while everything was deteriorating around us, we came together with the hope of making changes. And this is the result," she made a wide expansive gesture. "But it is, I hope, only a beginning."

One officer there, who had been in the Quality of Life

unit when it was formed and who was still in the precinct, walked up when she was finished. He said, "Rita, this is really like a miracle." He then announced to the others, "You would never believe what this block was like, seeing this now. It's like a miracle."

And in a way it was. Sometime later, Lieutenant Peter Pranzo announced the result of his long police clean-up campaign in a report which read:

"During the time period between 1979 and 1984, the 32nd Precinct Street Conditions Unit did conduct large scale arrest operations with mass or key arrests and many positive results:

A. During that time period, over 50 marijuana shops had been closed.
B. Approximately 300 outstanding warrants had been answered as a result of arrests effected by the unit.
C. The unit was responsible for approximately 50 percent of the overall arrests effected within the 32nd Precinct.
D. Three hundred vertical sweeps resulted in over 2,000 arrests with a conviction rate fluctuating between 80–85%.
E. Total street selling value of recovered narcotics by the unit was estimated at over $1,000,000.
F. A total of over 8,000 arrests were effected and 1,000 guns recovered.
G. The unit had been awarded Departmental Recognition for its members as a whole and individually, totalling over 300 citations for work in excellence, bravery or accomplished activity.

Some items which were recovered and seized by the unit are listed below:

Assorted Pills
U.S. Currency
Handguns, Shotgun and other Firearms
Foils/Containers Hashish
Knives
Bags of Angel Dust
Marijuana Cigarettes
Glassines of Heroin
Foils of Cocaine
Packs of Marijuana
Hypodermic Instruments
Drug Paraphernalia
Rounds of Ammunition
Scales
Point Blank Bullet Proof Vests and Flack Jackets

In April of 1984, the Malcolm X Apartment houses opened. Malcolm X on 143rd Street has one hundred apartments and the other building on West 144th street has fifty. Though it had been preceded by years of effort, the actual project had taken Rita only four years.

During this period she had faced seemingly insurmountable resistance from various politicians, drug dealers and, in the beginning, even the people she had sought to help. But Rita had persevered.

As she put it, at the ribbon cutting ceremony for the Malcolm X Houses: "Anger and frustration are meaningless emotions and they can be self-destructive. The only way we can move forward is to dream, plan and work for change.

"Those dreams deep inside us, which lie dormant for a while," she paused, "even a long while." Her eyes welled up with tears, "They don't always shrivel and die like raisins in the sun. Some like mine, like yours, are toughened, struggle to exist and gradually they mature and ripen into a determined will so that what once was fantasy can become a vision, a plan, and later reality."

For Rita, the block-wide celebration for the opening of the apartments was the culmination of that struggle. It was finally a real, not imaginary, victory. Here were the Malcolm X Houses, after all the fighting and planning. At one point there had seemed to be no end. "It was like a continuous sag," she had once explained. "You fixed one thing and another gets broken, like rebuilding a house."

But now there was an ending, a happy one. Rita invited all the politicians, the mayor, neighbors, everybody she could from all parts of the city. There was a big, big showing of important and ordinary people, all of whom saw this project as an example and encouragement for the things they wanted to do where they were.

Everyone for once agreed. This was unbelievable. Even Rita, herself, could hardly believe it was actually happening. But she did know it was only a beginning, as she called it, 'the first phase.'

She continued to dream and to plan.

Toward the end of 1984, Rita was awarded a Doctor of Human Letters Degree at Fordham. At the ceremony, the president of the school announced, "The Harlem Renaissance was a post-World War I movement that witnessed black writers, poets, painters and musicians joining together to protest in their own way against the quality of life for black Americans. Subsequent movements in the sixties and seventies resulted in the enactment of laws that enfranchised millions of Americans. Yet, many black Americans found life in their neighborhood not too different from before these movements.

"Rita Webb Smith, in an effort to provide a safe home for herself and her children, almost singlehandedly battled drug dealers and users, frequently endangering her own life in attempts to rid her surroundings of those forces that threatened to impair irrevocably the quality of life for her children and others' children. From this single-handed effort, she organized the block and neighborhood establishing the Community League of West 143rd Street, and the 143rd Street Community Preservation Group HSFC, Inc., a non-profit organization dedicated to preserving and stabilizing families through housing restoration. The result of Mrs. Smith's efforts can be seen in the $12 million Malcolm X Housing Rehabilitation Development on West 143rd Street and West 144th Street between Lenox Avenue and Adam Clayton Powell Boulevard. She was also founder of the Langston Hughes Child Development Center for pre-school children, the Division for Youth Volunteers, which provides self-help seminars for young people and, as Director of Parent Education, she developed educational material and seminars for women offenders at the Bedford Hills Correctional Facility.

"Fordham University has been proud to recognize Rita Webb Smith as an alumna-twice. After earning her Bachelor of Arts degree at The College at Lincoln Center, she enrolled in the Graduate School of Social Service from which she was not only awarded a Masters Degree in Social Work but was also selected by her fellow students as their graduation speaker. During her days as a Fordham student, Rita continued as a devoted and active mother to her seven children. This experience was captured in a film documentary on the survival of the black family and the resources needed to counter the stress of urban living.

"It is not possible for us at this time to cover adequately the full range of contributions to her community, contributions which were described last November when Mayor Koch and others paid tribute to this extraordinary woman on 'This is Your Life.'

"Mrs. Rita Webb Smith's activities may not match the earlier Harlem Renaissance in scope, but they represent a gigantic rebirth of a community that at one time saw despair and hopelessness as the only response to social conditions. Fordham University, as it honors Mrs. Smith today, joins a growing body of organizations and civic leaders in recognizing that even one concerned citizen can make a difference."

In early 1986 with the help of Councilman Fred Samuels and Deputy Commissioner Bob Davis, Rita and her preservation group were instrumental in opening on West 143rd street the Harriet Tubman Family Living Center to house former residents of Harlem who were homeless.

A few weeks later, Bob Davis, who was the Housing Preservation and Development Commissioner telephoned Rita excitedly. "Meet me in a half an hour at the preservation office. I have good news for you."

Rushing over, she saw Bob coming back from a walking tour. He gave her a big hug and then said, "Rita, listen, we're going to rebuild the whole block."

Rita, for once quieted by surprise said, "Really?"

"The city has a surplus in its budget," he continued. "It's all going to be done."

Then Rita looked up, smiling. "That's wonderful. That's really wonderful. Because what does it mean? It means freedom for all of us."

He smiled back and nodded. "It will be completed in 1990."

Rita threw back her head and laughed heartily. "Probably not if I know the city. But don't worry, I'll keep nudging it along."

Davis, like many other public officials, knew he could count on that.

What once seemed like an impossible dream was well on the road to materialization. But Rita's work was on-going. She began putting together a job-bank proposal. Through this new project, people in the community would acquire employment in areas such as carpentry and construction. Also, built into it would be an apprenticeship program which will help people to become licensed plumbers, carpenters, etc. Other jobs that will become available will be in management as well as in custodial positions.

Rita also formed a housing company which started out of an *ad hoc* group which is a non-profit organization called the 143rd Street Housing Preservation Company. This company cosponsored projects for which Rita wrote the proposals and tried to solicit the money. This housing company also provides tenant training and orientation. Rita's feeling was that these services set the tone for interest and appreciation of the place residents live.

Among the various community organizations Rita is also a member of the Precinct Council consisting of citizens and officers from that precinct. This type of group provides an open dialogue about the problems in the area, the efforts being made to alleviate those problems, as well as providing the support to other efforts being made for the progressive development of the community

In 1990, David Dinkins, now mayor of New York City, turned Rita's most expansive vision into reality when he announced that Mayor Edward Koch had given permission for a sixty-five million dollar project to begin the following year entitled Construction Management (Mana). The project called for revamping a ten block area in Harlem from 138th Street to 144th. "It will be tiered," Dinkins announced in a television broadcast on which he appeared with Rita and Bob Davis, "on work started by Rita Webb Smith."

After the television show ended, Rita, always the dreamer, always the realist, went home and began to formulate more concrete plans.

HOW?
THE PLAN

18

Miss Rita's Action Plan

"*T*he pushers are on your corner. You can see them as clearly as the nose on your face. Why can't the police? Why can't they merely swoop down in a bevy of police cars and surprise your local dope dealers? They could jump out with revolvers drawn just like on "Miami Vice," read 'em their rights, handcuff 'em, (maybe rough 'em up a little for good measure), and cart the scoundrels off to Central Booking never to be seen in your neighborhood again.

"Why can't the police just arrest all of them?

"I'll answer that question with a question and a statement. The question is, how do you compete with a profit of thousands of dollars a day? The statement is, the jails can't hold them all.

"These are the reasons that drug dealers are brazen enough to stalk our streets and doorways hawking their illegal wares. As a group, the young men and women who make their livings selling street drugs have taken over much of the American urban and suburban scene. Most are in their teens and early twenties (they can be considered fortunate if they live past age thirty), and are in the long run unemployable for obvious reasons. I describe them this way without the slightest fear of having this statement misconstrued; I am a black woman who lives in the best-known, and once the proudest black community in America. I am proud but I am practical, and I have eyes that see very well."

YOU ARE NOT ALONE: HOW TO START A DRUG CLEANUP—GETTING INTO ACTION

In most cases, if one chooses to stand by and not to do anything, the worst will happen anyway. In observing the invasion of the drug market, I found that many people were hit accidentally by stray bullets. The local people were also robbed, since robbery inevitably accompanies the arrival of drugs. Addicts are notorious thieves who steal to obtain and pawn goods for money to support their habits. In addition to the danger of accidentally being shot, or intentionally being robbed, we were subject to being burned out of our homes since there were fires almost every night in the abandoned buildings on the block.

In making assessments about getting action, you and your movement members must consider the following areas:

1. Help local residents overcome their fears. This can be done by working with a small *ad hoc* group to take care of some of the day-to-day problems. This committee can come out of block association members if there is such a group. To take back your streets, one thing you should request is more frequent patrolling by the police. Residents of the neighborhood are bound to notice this visible presence and begin to gain a greater sense of security.

2. Encourage people to negotiate with the system. The block association should distribute listed numbers for the various city services that people are most likely to call. Most times people don't call city agencies due to the fact that the telephone numbers are not readily available to them. When calling the police, advise residents not to give

their names, but to be able to provide pertinent information.

3. Get the system to respond to your needs. When you call or write, get correct names and addresses of agencies and persons who can assist you. Follow up on all complaints made to outside agencies. Invite members of city agencies to your meetings. Request informational brochures. Attend meetings at city agencies in reference to neighborhood problems. Get to know one particular person at each agency.

4. Focus on a rehabilitation plan for deteriorated buildings, parks or dumps in the area. Look at all sore thumbs in the block and other nuisances.

5. Develop a strategy to assist drug abusers to acquire help. You can contact the substance abuse agency in your area. They are more than happy to forward information and come out and talk to community groups. Local hospitals have drug abuse and maintenance programs . . . so, do eradicate the problem, but also try and help the victim.

6. Engage local organizations and churches in your efforts. Contact churches in your area, see what kind of assistance they can give. Perhaps they can offer rooms for meeting with community groups, etc. Perhaps they can do typing for the group or offer other resources.

7. Bring print attention to your efforts at making changes. There are many local community newspapers which can get your message out if you give them enough lead time. Write up your own press releases and send them to local newspapers. Try to get at least one reporter interested in your story. When prominent New York Daily News columnist Earl Caldwell became committed to helping us get publicity, he wrote articles at just the right times which led to citywide and later national exposure for 143rd Street and our takeback efforts. We couldn't have bought better advertising.

8. If you have ready-made shooting galleries and crack dens, once you've cleaned them out, put worthy tenants into the renovated housing with the help of local, state or federal government by changing abandoned housing into renovated housing.

To take back your block's housing stock, here are some steps to take:

A. Make a list of all abandoned houses on your street.

B. Investigate who owns these buildings at the office that keeps records of real estate ownership.

C. Research some of the city-funded housing programs that would fit the needs of your neighborhood. NOTE: Most cities have housing agencies where they list housing programs, public and private. Perhaps some of them will fit the needs of the neighborhood. Set up meetings with agency heads. Request surveys of the block for improvement of vacant lots, etc.

D. Request the sealing up of any abandoned, open buildings. These buildings are usually fire hazards or they can house the illegal drug trade and other illegal activities. The seal-up request can be made through the city housing agency or the local jurisdictional body.

E. Meet with the local police officials in reference to the drug trade and other problems pertaining to crime in the area. In most localities, the police department has a community affairs department. This is a good place to begin making contact.

F. Engage your local politicians in assisting in your efforts in helping to contact and pressure responsible agencies to do their jobs.

G. Set up your own protection network. Give your group members your general schedule, the time you go to work and return home. If you have had conflicts with any of the drug dealers or their family members, please have someone observe you while you are outside on the streets. If a confrontation occurs, all group members should be together. Do not confront anyone one-on-one. Let the law enforcement people handle such conflicts if they occur.

H. It's always a good move to acquire media attention. This will usually get attention placed on your particular problem. Everyone becomes much more responsive when the public eye is on them. Most agencies want to look good to the public. Remember that this is to your advantage.

I. Remember to look into resources for drug abusers. In a few cases, addicts will come to the local block association and ask for guidance. If none of the good guys ever offer help to drug abusers, there are plenty of pushers who will be glad to take them back as paying customers.

In getting into action you must remember what appears to be a weakness can actually be a strength in certain situations. Above all else, *YOU NEED EVERYBODY.* Each person can play an important role in taking a block back from the pushers if you'll only find out what that role is. Sometimes this becomes evident after many meetings with your committees; in most cases people grow and learn more about themselves while they're learning about everybody in the group.

Every pusher-squelching group needs people who can handle various aspects of the work. We found ours, young and old, bold and apprehensive, and you will too. A few of our members are categorized here so that you might spot talent that may help your movement.

"A Mouth That Roared"

On more than one occasion, Mrs. Johnson has confronted drug dealers in her hallway and pushed them out the door.

Note: Since she's so confrontational and bold, Mrs. Johnson made a good up-front person. This kind of participant is especially valuable if he or she is willing to assume responsibility.

"Eyes Galore"

Mrs. Curtis was about thirty-five years of age when we launched our movement. She had six children whom she raised alone. They ranged in age from four to seventeen. She worked as a part-time school crossing guard and as such, she saw a lot of the drug-dealing on the corner and up the block. When she joined the movement, she explained that she wanted to help, but that she did not want to be up front with her children being so vulnerable to reprisal and her being alone on the street while working.

Note: Mrs. Curtis is the kind of person who can give the group a great deal of information about what's going on especially since she is the type on who's corner all the activity is going on. This type of member is, in fact, very valuable because she can get physically closer to the criminal element without altering what they are engaged in doing.

"A Numbers Person"

Mr. Henry was about sixty-five years of age. He liked to sit out front on the stoop of his apartment building and enjoy the neighborhood. During the drug scourge, that was difficult for him to do. Mr. Henry had very keen eyesight. He was willing to take a background position to write down license plate numbers, descriptions of people, etc. But like Mrs. Curtis, Mr. Henry cautioned me that no one was ever to know that he was involved to the degree that he actually was. He didn't sit in the group meetings, but instead, gave his information privately.

Note: Not every member of your committee needs to or will want to speak out. Silent observers have their place too. Encourage people to give what they can.

"Middle Man

Shorty was about forty-five years old and was friendly enough that all the guys on the block liked him. He is a regular guy who even used to speak to the drug dealers. But he openly voiced his opinion to them that they needed to get off the block because their presence damaged the quality of life for everyone else. Shorty kept the pushers from coming into his building and doorway.

Note: Because he was such a good mediator between the pushers and the people in the movement, a lot of the residents would go to him for help with their day-to-day problems with the dope dealers. He was a negotiator and a good team player who could handle a variety of assignments.

In addition, there are several categories of neighbors who are sure to have vested interests in getting rid of drug dealers on local streets. In order to organize a community campaign to end pushing, it is a good idea to look at all of your options and use them.

UNDERSTANDING THE ELEMENTS OF DRUG DEALING: MODELS OF SUCCESS IN GETTING RID OF SELLERS AND BUYERS

To kill a weed, a gardener must have certain knowledge. While he or she can attempt to get rid of an unsightly plant by clipping off its above-ground growth, he or she will only succeed in eradicating weeds after she carefully pulls out, or poisons, the weed's tap root.

The correlation of this parallel with drug dealing is obvious. Unless a neighborhood purges the source of a drug sales operation, weeds have a way of sprouting again.

Taking low-level sellers off the scene is fine as a holding operation. In fact, you can get the ball rolling by starting your offensive this way. You need to cut off blatant street sales because they have a disastrous effect on your community—ruining the general morale of its people, attracting other crimes, even dragging down property values. To restore residents' confidence, and before you can even begin to turn the tide, you must see to it that the flunkies are swept out.

But that alone is nothing more than a quick-fix for the endemic, entrenched drug site. New York City police estimated that in one Lower East Side neighborhood, there were fifteen dealers waiting to replace each pusher who was arrested. There are more than 100,000 felony and misdemeanor drug arrests in the city each year. Yet only one out of three persons arrested on felony narcotics charges in New York is even indicted, according to the state's division of criminal justice services, because suspects plea bargain and admit to lesser crimes.

Obviously, you are not going to get prison sentences

for all the guys dealing on your block. But what I did in Harlem and what you are fully capable of doing (with help) is to snatch out the root—meaning having your local drug dealing site disrupted and thereby put out of business. To prove this to you, let's de-mystify the way that all drug sale operations are conducted. Armed with this information, you can interrupt the cycle that allows drug sellers and buyers to connect.

Whether it's a sprawling, multinational network or the single-seller practice, there are ultimately only four elements involved in any drug dealing: a seller, a drug, a location and a buyer. When you understand that an operation consists of these individual elements, you have much less to confuse you. As in any military strategy, the objective thus becomes disrupting the enemy by striking at his vulnerable points.

1) The Seller

At the outset, let me just declare for the record that drug dealers are criminals. Despite any of our benevolent leanings, while remaining cognizant of the wrongs visited upon many Americans by a harsh, racist society, no one has to violate laws forbidding possession and sale of narcotics.

Drug dealing is neither benign nor victimless. It's violent and virulent. I'm still chilled at how one seven year old Newark, New Jersey boy on the way home from school was grabbed by grown men who told him to hold their drugs while they stood on the corner and did business. The reason they forced him to stand there holding their narcotics was that, as a youngster, he wouldn't be suspected of carrying, nor could they be arrested for possession. They could not have cared less that the little boy was frightened out of his wits. You don't call that being victimized by pushers?

Since the dealer is the most important element in the

drug dealing process, the most attention must be paid to his personality and *modus operandi.* Among his most vulnerable points are: fear of discovery, fear of arrest and conviction, fear of disruption or loss of business and fear of community reprisal.

What you hope to effect are police arrests. To facilitate that, you need to know what a police arrest for drugs is. There are several types of arrest. There's The Observation Sale: police see a sale take place and arrest the dealer and possibly the buyer. There's The Buy-And-Bust: an undercover police officer disguises as a person who wants to buy drugs, actually purchases a quantity of them as evidence, then another officer arrests the sellers. And, of course, as occurred on 143rd Street there are the Sweep Arrests where numbers of officers make a mass arrest of any number of suspects.

In all instances, police must have probable cause to make an arrest. You're not facing reality if you fail to understand this—the police are ten times less likely to accept your view of "obvious" drug selling as you are. "How do you know *what* they're selling?" they will ask you.

You obtain probable cause by watching recurring transactions and documenting the details to prove drugs were sold. When armed with information, undercover police can buy the drug and arrest the culprit.

Become more aware of agencies such as the Crime Victim Services Bureau. We were able to get this agency to come in and put locks on all the apartment doors and install special locks for senior citizens.

Contact the district attorney's office. We gave officials in this office information regarding the dealers. At times, since it is sometimes hard to get the dealers on drug charges, the district attorney's office could focus on getting the dealers who had committed other crimes off the streets. This approach produced some good results with one dealer getting a prison sentence of thirty years for murder. One of the policemen with whom the group was working gathered the evidence against this dealer with the group's help.

It was a new phenomenon for the police to have the community working with them. That was rare in our area. The police were able to do a better job once they were given the right kind of information, especially in the area of description, by the people in the neighborhood.

The police taught the people of the neighborhood to be observant and precise in their descriptions of suspicious persons or acts. The people learned descriptions; to describe what the dealers were wearing, looking to see where they hid the drugs and how.

In other words, a number of things can work together successfully and did in our case: all the work with the district attorney's office, the victims services agency, the police sweeps, the arrests, finding and confiscating the drugs to hit the dealers' economics. The drug dealers could not help but feel this pressure.

2) The Drugs

In New York state, persons who possess and/or sell controlled substances are "committing criminal offenses against the public health and morals." The controlled substances are marijuana, concentrated cannabis, narcotic drugs or preparations, hallucinogens, stimulants, dangerous depressants or depressants. Since crack cocaine is the current drug of choice, Cocaine can serve as an example. Cocaine is classified as a narcotic. Possession of a controlled substance is at least a misdemeanor, possession of more then an eighth ounce of cocaine, for instance, is a felony. So is sale.

Concrete evidence of the presence of a narcotic for sale is often the least reliable of the vulnerable points. Seasoned sellers use all sorts of subterfuge to keep from handling actual substances or to keep from handling large enough quantities to warrant arrest. Marijuana dealers may hold oregano, coke dealers just about any harmless white powder.

Being sure a dealer is in fact holding the real McCoy when the police corner him is the key. If you get enough information to the police, they should eventually be able to make the undercover arrest that will make the case.

3) Location

The fact that drug dealing is done in your neighborhood is really the reason you're fed up in the first place, isn't it? In my case, had one major dealer, Victor and his Black Sunday boys, gotten off the block and gone down by the river as I early on suggested to him, I wouldn't have been as worried about them. Locations to sell drugs are a dime a dozen. Some operations change apartments as often as once a day. We know we can't scour the earth of narcotics, but Lord knows we don't want them sold on our doorsteps.

4) The Buyer

They whys and wherefores of this problem is a whole other subject. Let it suffice to say this self-destructive element indicates a nationwide epidemic is on the rise.

LEGAL STEPS TO RID YOUR STREETS OF DRUGS

A. "Getting Evictions"

While your group is reclaiming your street, you must also get the traffic out of its hiding places as well. Unless you can eliminate the source, you don't stand much of a chance of clearing away undesirables and the crimes they foster.

Eviction of dealers is the answer. If a drug operation has gone behind closed doors, so must you, at least figuratively, by leading the authorities there to rout the scoundrels.

There are now widely-spread methods for terminating the leases of tenants whose apartments are used to sell narcotics. In April, 1989, the United States Secretary of Housing and Urban Development, Jack Kemp, streamlined the process of evicting tenants in public housing. Since then, a tenant, guest or family member who makes, sells or uses drugs or who possesses them with those intentions can be sent packing without a lengthy hearing by the housing officials. In other words, now they can kick your butt directly out of there, and then you can fight it out in court, if you choose to do so.

The 1988-enacted Federal Public Housing Drug Elimination Act is a good tool for throwing traffickers out of the projects. In recent years, federal housing projects in Boston, Cleveland, New York City, Chicago and even Portsmouth, Virginia, have used the law to some benefit. The stipulation allows federal marshals to seize an apartment where undercover agents make two confirmed drug buys. Cleveland, for instance, used this law to get rid of nearly two hundred residents for drugs, almost seventy-five percent of the total two hundred sixty persons the housing authority evicted in a recent year. Chicago's housing authority attempted to evict one hundred ninety-two tenants in one ten-month period in 1989; one-third were drug-related.

Even where the percentages aren't quite as high, a tough law with teeth in it can produce the needed bite. "All you need is one crack house," said an official of Portsmouth's public housing agency, "and you've got a problem."

Fortunately, the private sector is getting involved too. According to a *New York Times* article, at least one landlord in town also has a no-drug policy. After getting advice from the state attorney, a Portsmouth apartment mogul with nearly twenty-four hundred apartment units, notified his renters that they would be evicted if they, or someone in their household, are arrested for a drug-related offense. To enforce his edict, on a regular basis, he pores over the police department's narcotics arrest printouts.

Before the 1980's, using such a legal tactic was virtually unheard of to the police, landlords, or public housing officials. But, unbelievably, in the Big Apple, the statute that puts a going spell on drug traffickers was written in 1840. Was that perhaps because pre-Civil War lawmakers had drug dealers wresting neighborhoods from decent folks? No, not exactly. The problem back in the mid-ninteenth Century was a little more sensual. The trade in question back then was prostitution. Hence the statute's monicker, "The Bawdy House Law."

Anyone living within two hundred feet of a New York City house where illegal trade, business or manufacture activity takes place can file the 'bawdy house' complaint, technically known as *Section 715 of New York's Real Property Actions and Proceedings Law*. In fact, to bring about the eviction of an occupant, you don't even have to depend upon the cooperation of the building's landlord. The law says that the plaintiff can be awarded the cost of his legal troubles *from the landlord.* You don't have to have a conviction, just an arrest. The opportunity for abuse, therefore, exists.

In 1989, the Oakland police department sued more than one hundred homeowners under a California statute that lets cities bring actions punishable by up to $25,000 in fines against residents whose homes were public nuisances. Moreover, Oakland actually had the right to demolish buildings where there had been drug sales.

As a matter of fact, how would you like to even recoup some money from building owners whose drug dealing tenants have caused you so much grief?

The most encouraging news on evicting dealers comes from Berkeley, California, where fifteen citizens, fed up with a crack house on their block, filed a small-claims suit against the building's unresponsive landlord. In the suit, they charged that the landlord's crack house was a public nuisance because its clients brought increased auto traffic, gunfire, condoms, syringes and fast food litter, and they made the residents afraid to use their own street. In what's been called a landmark decision for reclaiming streets, a judge awarded the plaintiffs $1,000 each. The shocked landlord then gave the tenants a three-day eviction notice after which he evicted the tenants. Of course, that's the step he should have taken in the first place after the neighbors brought him proof his house was a site for illegal trade.

"At no point did we confront the drug dealers. It's a business, and property-management problem. We sued the absentee owner as a bad manager. The secret is to collectively do it. We even had an eight month old baby sue because her mother couldn't safely walk her down the street in her carriage," says Molly Wetzel, the progenitor of the Berkeley group that sued. "Small claims in California is very helpful."

284

Berkeley has some of the strictest rent control laws in the nation. No lawyers are needed or even allowed in the small claims process. A person pays $4 to file the complaint. Within thirty days, if a judge hasn't given you a ruling, he can order an investigation. After forty-five days, he usually hands down his ruling.

The Berkeley take-backers had struggled for almost two years to clean up the crack house, countless times notifying police and the building's owner. Yet only six months after they filed, they cleared out the drug house dealers and collected the money.

After this stinging weapon to evict pushers was publicized, the phone didn't stop ringing at Molly Wetzel's home. Molly, a single mother, had started the Francisco Community Group after a drug user near the crack house grabbed her teenage son. The addict put a gun to her son's head, threatening to blow it off if the kid didn't give him money. Her terrified son rifled his pockets to produce any loose ransom he could trade for his life. All he had was fifty-five cents. The dealer looked at it in disgust and snatched it from the boy but let him live.

Molly and three full time trainers have developed Safe Streets Now, a step-by-step approach to remove drug houses from rental property. When Wetzel comes to a city, she tailors a community action book to be block-by-block site-specific. She also orients the court system so those in the local judicial system will know how to react with dozens of community activists come to them with nuisance complaints. "It turns the victims into the liberators," Molly emphasizes.

More than eighteen hundred grassroots organizations are fighting drugs in the major American cities, according to the National Center for Neighborhood Enterprises.

On a rainy Saturday morning in March, 1988, a seminar given in New York's John Jay College drew nearly two hundred citizens representing a purported four thousand persons from some of those blockwatch groups and community agencies.

Scores of participants stood up and spilled out sordid tales of how drug dealing had blighted blocks and, in some cases, whole neighborhoods. But the most memorable story by far was that told by a young black woman named Marie Christopher.

"If the people in the community decide they want change in their community, it's usually done much fairer," says Marie Christopher.

Shy, weak-voiced Marie Christopher does not look like a woman who could take on a shotgun-brandishing drug dealer, yet to see this stylish, thirtyish lady, one would also probably not assign her as a formerly homeless person either. Yet, she once was; forced out into the streets of Spanish Harlem in 1983 after a group of drug dealers torched the building in which Marie lived because their competitors lived there also. A single mother who attended college, she knew that the pushers were operating in her tenement apartment building. She had chosen not to challenge their right to sell there because she had two sons to protect. She thought she should look the other way.

But once the intentional blaze destroyed her place, Marie had no choice but to send her children to live with her mother while she roamed New York shelterless.

Seven months later, Marie found a new home in the Pueblo Nuevo Apartments on Manhattan's Lower East Side. Yet just two years later Marie recognized the unmistakable signs of drug-selling from a neighborhood apartment. Up to one hundred seventy-four visitors a night visited the drug apartment, according to the record book kept by security guards.

The illegal operation brought its attendant groups of

belligerent customers who smoked their crack in the hallways and even jumped residents for money. Marie's previous experience haunted her thoughts.

Policemen and city officials rarely instruct citizens who are being harassed to fight back. Citizens are all too aware of the police department's limitations. Marie was aware, but her 1986 adversity caused Marie to be introduced to herself and to an inherent courage. She made the choice—I'll fight back.

But she knew she couldn't fight alone. Marie cajoled her building's neighbors into coming to tenant meetings to discuss how to get rid of the building's crack dealer. He was a paraplegic who rode around in his wheelchair with a shotgun under the blanket on his lap.

At her urging, the local police precinct assigned nine beat cops to restore order in Pueblo Nuevo. She and her neighbors also took their protest to management, complaining that the security company that had been guarding the complex was inefficient. Management fired the old company and contracted with a new one. And in a satisfying case of "back at you," the residents nearly broke their faces every time a customer of the dealer showed up—escorted to his apartment by New York Police Department lieutenant Michael Walsh or his officers. Walsh used the police's *right-to-inquiry-plus-escort* stipulation, which not only allowed him to ask the pusher's visitors for ID, and take them to the dealer's door but even to wait for them and escort them out.

"Trust me, nobody wants to be escorted to their drug dealer's door," Marie chuckles. "Besides it does more than just deter the customers. It gives the police the opportunity to see who's buying drugs so that if they see the person a week later in another location, they have a good idea who's buying drugs and where the new spot is."

But the dealer wasn't laughing. He leveled threats at several residents he thought were involved in the campaign

to oust him. It was alleged he put out a $1,000 murder con-
tract for the person who had plastered an anti-crack poster
on his door and those of all the other residents they suspected of using or selling drugs with him.

Finally, one night a gunshot was reported from his
room. The police came with a warrant, searched the apartment, and upon finding large quantities of crack, cash and
weapons, arrested the dealer on possession and sales
charges. While out on bail, he was caught selling narcotics
again. This time the judge waived the man's right to bail
and got right to the business of throwing the book at the
guy. He was arraigned and sentenced to between four-and-
one-half to nine years in prison.

Marie stresses, however, that the only way to make
sure that dealers get time is to stay involved with the district attorney during the preparation of the case. The D.A.'s
community affairs office can be particularly helpful.

Ever since her dramatic success over her area's main
drug dealer, Marie Christopher has been a national media
star for the take-back movement. She's also become a national consultant: a member of the Steering Committee for
a Drug-Free New York, and a consultant to the Citizens
Committee of New York's National Dissemination Project.
Marie goes all over the United States speaking and training
groups to use the law to reclaim their communities.

Among her advice, for instance, is that besides local
variations of the bawdy house or padlock laws, citizens can
now use what are called narcotics eviction programs. Prove
to a district attorney that a landlord is aware of drug sales
in his building, prove he refuses to do anything about it and
you can charge him with conspiracy. He can be sentenced
to a stiff fine, to jail or even have his property turned over
for forfeiture.

Also, "unless you keep up a relationship at the precinct, you don't get the service. Meet police community affairs people and the special tactics people," Marie says.

And getting rid of a local bad guy doesn't always end the problems, either. She and her neighbors now have a new problem called the Rainbow Drug Project-thirteen year old kids who are commissioned to deal on her street, but not in the apartments.

B. "Grass Roots Movements To Stop Street Sales"

Marie and I wrested back patches of Manhattan, although, to be sure, there are thousands of enemy-occupied blocks still to be reclaimed. The scourge also rages in Brooklyn, a thriving "outer" borough of New York City, but a few years ago, its perpetrators were given notice to keep dope from crossing at least one certain green sidewalk painted line.

"You cannot let your fear stop you from doing what you have to do," explains a Sunni Muslim who closed a bevy of crack houses within four blocks of his mosque. The imam or minister, Siraj Wahaj, proved true to his word when he led a forty-day vigil against drug dealing near Masjid At-Taqwa in the Bedford Stuyvesant section of Brooklyn. The Muslims' campaign is to be expecially applauded because it was an example of black men taking the initiative.

Masjid At-Taqwa was established in 1981 by a handful of black American Muslims who'd become disenchanted with the Nation of Islam after Elijah Muhammad died. Most of them had been attracted to the American version of Islam because Muslims, epitomized by the prototype, Malcolm X, were militant about protecting their people. Eventually, however, the members of this group had matured to an orthodox strain of Islam, known as Sunni, that emphasized truth, peacefulness with all men, but self-defense

289

when necessary. The At-Taqwa community numbered some two hundred fifty persons. Several members purchased small storefronts from the city and opened businesses in property on Bedford Avenue.

But the commercial strips buttressing Bedford-Stuyvesant, the predominantly black neighborhood of attractive three-story single-family brownstones made famous in Spike Lee's movie, *Do the Right Thing*, were in effect nightly shopping centers for persons seeking narcotics. On the sidewalks where Muslim men and women were writing their life stories, dealers chased down customers by scurrying over to passing cars.

In January of 1987, the landlord of an apartment building pleaded with Imam Wahhaj to help him evict squatters who were living in and selling drugs on his property, yet weren't even paying rent. Talal Jaber, the landlord, had gotten nowhere after seven complaints to police. Later that month, thirty of the At-Taqwa Muslims—solemn, bearded, broad shouldered African American men from the same tough streets as the drug pushers—knocked on the door of an apartment they identified as the base for dealers and drug-using prostitutes. They confronted the ten people inside.

After the Muslims told the squatters to leave, they did, but amazingly had the gall to notify police that the Muslims had threatened them with weapons. Eventually five of the Muslims were arrested for burglary, menacing and possession of weapons, a shotgun, a handgun and knives. They spent three days in jail and were sentenced to probation.

A year later, while Wahhaj and four other At-Taqwa men awaited trial on felony and misdemeanor charges, they mounted an ingenious stance to make an even bigger impact on safer, drug-free streets.

Through a series of meetings with the New York Police Department's Brooklyn Patrol North unit, Wahhaj arranged for police to make an initial sweep of three blocks surrounding his masjid. "Hit every area hard to get the pushers out for a while. After that, we'll patrol on our own for forty days," Commanding Officer Rayford recalls Wahhaj saying.

On a cold, winter night, the police raided twelve suspected crack houses in the vicinity of the masjid and locked up thirty-three people. The next day, fifteen Muslim men made their rounds of the neighboring blocks carrying walkie-talkies and striding together in pairs. For forty days and forty nights (a lovely symbolic reference to events spiritual) the At-Taqwa patrol manned their streets. No one could mistake their identities—they wore distinctive knit kufis on their heads, and often wore long, Arab tunics beneath their contemporary ski jackets. And none of the pushers could question the Muslims' hard-headed resolution. They began by walking up to the pushers who were handing out drugs and boldly announcing to then, "You can't do business here any more. We suggest that you don't sell them at all, but you definitely can't sell them here."

Wahhaj claimed that his vigil was commanded in the Koran in that its scriptures say, "Enjoin the good and forbid the evil." The results of the forty-day patrol were striking, as blatant merchandising of drugs slowed, then halted. Almost as gratifying as the met goal, though, was a comment that a drug dealer made to Wahhaj when he told him, "Brother, you're killing me, but I know it's something that has to be done."

Chief Rayford explains, "I don't want to suggest that everyone can do what the At-Taqwa community did. They were a particularly committed group. There's risk involved. But in unity there is safety. Pushers choose the line of least resistance. They shy away from communities that are well-organized with block associations."

If you and other women have no choice but to make a stand alone, I am proof that God will help you stay the fight. But wherever possible, I like to see a movement made up of men as well as women in a community confronting the mostly male drug dealers.

In Kansas City, Missouri, an ex-police detective named Alvin Brooks, himself nearly sixty years old, recruits men from his age group down to those in their twenties to help clean crack houses. His band also includes female victims of sexual assaults, ex-drug users and ex-alcoholics and professionals. These persons have mitigated the risk of coming outside and being identified with a cause they would die for, rather than living imprisoned behind triple-locked doors and barred windows.

Brooks admits that the job of closing crack houses is risky; and he ought to know. In one eight-month period, he says that his Ad Hoc Group Against Crime helped Kansas City police and prosecutors shut down fifty-four crack houses.

With some one hundred members, Brooks has held more than three hundred drug rallies, mostly on turf usurped by pushers. He says he has received only insignificant heckling and no threats. "We know what we're doing is risky, but you take a greater risk by not doing anything," he explains. "The drug dealers are here only as long as you allow them."

Alvin has made what can be considered a big-time commitment. His is not the kind of involvement that everyone can afford. Not only is he the director of the Kansas City Human Relations Department, but, for thirteen years, he's compiled an extracurricular league table that is formidable; sessions teaching persons how the criminal justice system operates, a secret witness hotline, school rallies. The Ad Hoc'ers are closely connected to a second organization Brooks helped start in 1987, Black Men Together. Those men take kids to sporting events and rout any dealers by standing in groups next to any on-site dealers.

292

The members are in the great tradition of take-backers in that they use dramatic symbols—gimmicks, if you will—to attract the attention of both the ne'er-do-wells and the locals who've heretofore tried to look the other way. For their rallies, Brooks and Company have borrowed a wooden coffin from a mortuary and gotten police to block off the streets where stand the crack houses. As speaker after speaker uses a battery-operated bullhorn to harangue the felons operating inside, the other members of the Ad Hoc team hand out fliers to passersby to involve them in the fight. Their strategy is to close the sites of illegal sales, or at least keep the dealers moving. Brooks says that when they can't set up infrastructures, the pushers are vulnerable.

In addition, anytime there's a murder in the community, the group convenes a 6 p.m. vigil at the murder scene, complete with prayers, songs and eulogy. "Unless God was helping us," says Brooks, "I don't think any of us believe we could be successful." Besides having this endorsement from the highest authority, Brooks acknowledges that the mayor and city council of Kansas City back him to the hilt.

In Hollywood, California (as *USA Today* reported it, "just six blocks away from Grauman's Chinese Theater, the world's most famous movie house") pushers used to press drivers in passing cars to buy. The Hollywood Sentinels, a group of local folks who banded together to end the practice, has put a big dent in their trade.

First, resident Debbie Wehbe went with her husband to sessions given by police and the Guardian Angels on how to make citizens' arrests. Armed with this practical knowledge, they attacked the pushers in a way that terrifies those who are used to just taking over neighborhoods—they confronted them in numbers. Debbie and her buddies sallied right up to the dealers' faces, asking them "What are you doing here? This is our area, so go back where you came from."

The Sentinels met the perpetrators head-on and have run them out. Of course, they're under no illusions that their neighborhood is not prime turf for drug sales in the future, but they plan to stay vigilant. I'm proud that Debbie and groups like hers are part of what she sees as a "nation-wide wave."

Obviously, it is my opinion that these kinds of grass-roots confronters are our best salvation from the junkies gone buggy over the ephemeral gratification of cocaine highs or heroin heavens. Nevertheless, it seems amusing that she and millions like her think that citizens taking back their streets is new. "It's something we should have been doing ten years ago, but we didn't," she says.

"Some of us did, my dear. Some of us did."